BEHIND THE DOORS
OF REALITY

BEHIND THE DOORS
OF REALITY

✦

TEARS OF A MILITARY WIFE

A MOTHER'S TESTIMONIAL

Jessie Thompson

iUniverse, Inc.
New York Lincoln Shanghai

BEHIND THE DOORS OF REALITY
TEARS OF A MILITARY WIFE

iUniverse books may be ordered through booksellers or by contacting:

iUniverse
2021 Pine Lake Road, Suite 100
Lincoln, NE 68512
www.iuniverse.com
1-800-Authors (1-800-288-4677)

ISBN-13: 978-0-595-39236-0 (pbk)
ISBN-13: 978-0-595-83628-4 (ebk)
ISBN-10: 0-595-39236-9 (pbk)
ISBN-10: 0-595-83628-3 (ebk)

Printed in the United States of America

This book is dedicated to my son Phillipe and my grandson Dwayne with special thanks to Mario, Tina and Ruby.

Remember that no experience in life is a wasted experience. Sometimes life's table serves us things that we'd prefer not to have to deal with, but as we travel down life's road, may it be rocky or smooth, these experiences develops wisdom that adds light for our path, so let not your heart be troubled, neither let it be afraid, we will understand it better by and by.

Contents

If you or someone you know is in a domestic violence situation contact:

National Crisis Hotline
(800) 779-SAFE or (800) 787-3224
(7233)

Samartian House Crisis Hotline
(757) 430-2121

Domestic Violence Hotline
(800) 621-HOPE
(4673)

Crime Victims Hotline
(866) 689-HELP
(4357)

http:www.ndvh.org

http:www.gmdvp.org

PREFACE

During our search for the perfect mate we realize that relationships are easy to develop but difficult to legally alleviate. We sometimes find ourselves in uncomfortable and uncompromising situations with a mate who insists upon causing physical, mental and emotional distress. With the onset of misery, depression, anger, uncertainty and desperation we diligently seek refuge in whatever area that we could find support.

However, while domestic violence has become an epidemic in the world of relationships it is a subject that many people choose not to acknowledge simply because there are very few laws established for their protection. Most people release the issue and withdraw the charges immediately after the drama subsides.

In today's world men as well as women, have had some experiences with a controlling mate and find themselves in a situation where hostility is introduced to the rebellious partner. So many people have been battered, marred and murdered while waiting for someone to figure out what legal rights the victim holds in these situations. If we are going to free society of these behaviors, we must begin to get serious about finding ways to alert the lawmakers that we are tired and refuse to accept it anymore. We must press and hold charges against our attackers even if it is their first offense. There is no excuse for these behaviors and the only ones who can dissipate these crimes are the victims and family members.

BOOK DESCRIPTION

Behind the doors of reality—Tears of a military wife begins by telling a provocative story about a woman who single-handedly raise her children in the fast-paced lifestyle of New York City. It also gives a first hand eyewitness into the lives of several military spouses and the problems that they encounter as they travel in and out of the United States with their husbands.

Justice for a ladybug is an individual story of its own about a young woman who marries her high school sweetheart who intentionally conspire a scheme that ensnares her into his web of brutality and leaves her gasping for her last chances of life.

As you gather a close up view of the seriousness of domestic violence, this story will leave you wondering if society is really doing enough to absolve the world of this crime that many people become monotonously subjected to.

You will encounter never-ending suspense as you discover what strongholds keep this author entrusting in God and what prophecies are sent to comforter, lead, motivate and encourage her through the daily trials of life.

AS I WAIT

So often my patience is short
there are so many things that I don't understand
It seems that the whole world is against me
and I'm climbing a mountain of dry sand

It seems the harder I try
the deeper I sink
The higher I reach
the less I receive

The more I pray
the more I stray
Even when I think I'm strong
it seems impossible to go on

I came to Virginia
with a hope and a dream
But it seems that I have been stripped
of every single thing

My daughter has been murdered
because of another's heartless act
My family ripped apart
my soul is under attack

Sometimes I don't care
should I live or should I die

All I know is that
I no longer want to cry

In the midst of daily trying times
I try to hold tight onto my faith
cause in the end I know
that victory awaits

Father, you said
No weapons formed against me shall prosper
You said you'd make my enemies my footstool
You said you would fight my battles
if I just stand still

Now I'm standing here
with my hands in the air
Without an ounce of strength left
wondering if anybody really cares

I know that one day
my victory will come, but
I ask again as I dry another tear
Lord, where do I go from here?

I have forgiven, confessed and prayed
even for those who snicker at my pain
Lord, bless me with patience and strength
to stand strong as I wait

LABOR DAY

I knew that today was going to be the greatest day of my life. It didn't matter that I lived in a city that was heavily polluted, heavily congested and extremely noisy because right now the only thing that I am concentrating on is the puddle of water that lie beneath my feet. I was standing at the counter of Burger King ordering my breakfast when I felt the warm gush flow down my legs and onto the floor. Feeling a little embarrassed, yet delighted I quickly grabbed my bag and headed out the door for the sixteen-block walk back home. I didn't care what the people in line behind me thought because I knew that my baby was on the way. My imagination quickly raced into tomorrow with thoughts of how I would be holding the most amazing and greatest gift that God could have ever blessed me with. Hoping and praying for a girl, I was determined that I was not going to exaggerate this moment although I'd heard countless stories about the horrors of childbirth. The only thing that matters to me at this moment is the thought of knowing that today is the day that my whole world will be changed forever. I wanted to skip and I wanted to leap all the way back, but my condition was not allowing me to do that. It was just a few months ago that I would hold my stomach and declare "Chelle's woke" with every idle and drastic movement of the little creature that was growing inside of me and now my dream is about to become a reality.

When I reached the house I immediately began searching the yellow pages for the telephone number to the Red Cross. My husband was in the military, stationed in Balmholder, Germany and I needed to let him know that the time has come. How I wished he could be here to share this moment with me, but I knew that it was a huge possibility that he would not make it here in time. Still, I was determined that I would try and hold out for as long as I could while giving him travel time. I didn't tell anyone else about my encounter at Burger King because I didn't want anyone to try and talk me into going to the hospital yet, so I went through the day as normal as I could. I tightly clinched my teeth and pretended to smile with every strike of pain while trying my best to hang in there a little while longer.

The sun had begun to set when I finally decided that I couldn't hold out any longer. I confessed. Could someone please get me to the hospital I blurted in a loud voice? Panic set within everyone but me. My cousin grabbed the bag that I had previously packed. The little pink outfit that lay across the top would soon be filled. The blue outfit that lied beneath was just in case God didn't hear my prayers. My sister grabbed me by the arm and everyone was heading for the door. At first everything seemed comical including the moment when we walked onto the Labor and Delivery ward, my sister on the left, being eight months pregnant herself and my cousin on the right, seven month along. I couldn't help but burst into laughter at the expression on the nurse's face when my sister cried out "the baby is coming". I guess I had endured so much pain all day that this moment didn't seem too troublesome at all. I lay there watching the clock for hours wondering when it would all be over. I listened as people wailed and cried, screamed and cursed, hollered and sworn. Finally I heard those magic words "it's a girl!" Thank you Lord was all I could reply. Thank you, Thank you, Thank you.

I know that every mother thinks her child is the most beautiful child ever born, but I tell you, LaChelle really was. She weighed in at seven pounds of pure delight with a head full of thick black, curly hair. My entire soul was enlightened to know that my Ladybug had finally arrived. I spent hours counting all ten toes and all ten fingers while running my fingers across her tiny rib cage as I made account for every single little bone. I turned her upside down, flipped her over and over adoring every inch of that little body. I didn't consider myself much of a Christian at that time, but I knew that God had truly blessed me on this day. Chelle grew up to be a very happy, high-spirited child and as she grew she always made it a point to let me know that I was her favorite person in the whole world. At four years old she loved to play trick on me. I often think of the time when I was in the kitchen cooking while she and her brother Philip napped in the other room, I was just about to pour the boiling water from the spaghetti into the strainer when suddenly a small body jumped from behind the wall and screamed "Boo". She was giggling so hard that she lost control of her little body and began sliding down the wall to the floor. The idea of startling me nearly tickled her to death, yet there I stood holding my chest and thanking God that I didn't drop that pot.

Everyone in the family held a special place in her heart and she loved each of us in a special but separate way. Her three-year-old brother was not only her ideal playmate but also the person that she nurtured and protected as much as she could with the motherly nature that God instilled within her. As she was growing up that nature got her into one fight after another while trying to protect someone else for some reason or another.

JUST BEING MOM

After ten years of marriage and one year of separation I found myself back in New York alone trying to raise my two children as a single parent. That wasn't what bothered me because during the time that I was married, I was a married/single parent anyway. But now my children have been relocated to a city of unruly, uncontrollable and misbehaved peers. Their backgrounds had nurtured them into being the military brats that they were and I wasn't sure if they could handle this drastic change. I had already informed them upon what they were about to face with hopes that they could adjust. They understood that in New York you have to literally, physically fight your way through the school system in order to survive. It was breaking my heart to know that I had to subject my children into this type of lifestyle. I knew that they were scared and so was I, but I didn't have much of a choice. Thank God, it did not take long for them to alter and they soon realized that not only did they have to fight with other students, but then after sitting up half the night struggling to complete assignments, we still had to verbally fight with the teacher for a decent grade just so that they could pass to the next grade. Because of my own childhood experiences, I really didn't have much respect for the New York school system anyway. With LaChelle being the most aggressive and Philip being her protector, they narrowly escaped the harsh reality of the New York Department of Education.

Thank God that it took only one short month to find employment because I felt that I needed financial stability to prepare myself for the times when the actions of my children would be out of my control; you know, those teenage years, those I know it all years, those I'm grown and you can't tell me what to do years. They were well aware that I had no other choice but to maintain a full-time job to pay the bills and keep a roof over our heads, while receiving the bare minimum for child support. They also knew that I couldn't afford to take time off work to chase them and just like many children of single-parent households, my children had the opportunity to use the apartment to cut school, smoke, hang out with friends, prepare meals, or basically do whatever they decided to during the hours that I was working. They quickly learned to call me at a certain time to lead me to believe that they were just coming home from school even if they weren't; but what my children did not know was my methods for prevention. They did not know how creative I was in finding ways to keep up with their whereabouts.

The high school that LaChelle attended was located within walking distance of my employment and she would sometimes stop by on her way home to say hello. This was one of the combinations that she tried when she wanted to check my daily activities. These were the days in which I took the initiative to wait for her to leave before taking advantage of scheduled time off. This gave me the opportunity to, at their unawareness, follow them and verify their daily schedule in order that I may know what their involvements were, what type of friends they associated with and what their after-school activities involved. Upon many occasions they were puzzled about how I obtained the information that I possessed although they became cautious each time they telephoned my job and connected to my voicemail. LaChelle finally figured out my methods the Friday that she came by the office and found that I had been out on vacation all week.

One of the most important things to me while raising my children was teaching them to be independent leaders of society. My fears were placed on hold one day when Philip came into the house from the playground unexpectedly, headed directly for his room, turned on the television and sat quietly in front of it. I knew that something was on his mind and it was obvious that he did not want to share with me at this moment, therefore I just allowed him to be alone with his thoughts for a while. Eventually he fell asleep and I forgot to ask him about it later as he grabbed his bicycle and headed for the playground again. We didn't live in the best of neighborhoods and sometimes my children would befriend with people that wasn't exactly good influences. Even then, with guidance, I allowed them to make their final choice of friends. The streetlights had come on and that was the only time clock that my children needed to know when to come inside for the evening. We had already finished dinner and I was in the process of washing dishes when I heard a knock on the door. "Who is it", I responded as the neighbor identified herself politely. As I opened the door Candice stood with her coat across her arm and pocketbook over her shoulder. It was obvious that she was going somewhere and from the look on her face I knew that she needed a favor from me. She began by telling me that her son had been arrested today and she needed a ride to the precinct to retrieve him. It seemed that he, Philip and a few other boys had rode their bicycles to the mall and as the other boys went on a shoplifting spree Philip decided to separate himself and head for home. While I sympathized with her, I was assured and delighted to know that Philip was mentally strong enough not to fall into the lap of peer pressure.

Because of the close relationship that I held with my children, many of the other children in the neighborhood acclaimed me as the coolest mom in the neighborhood, not because I thought I was cool, but because my children could confide in me things that other children wouldn't dare tell their parents. Surprisingly my children were proud to know that they had the coolest mom in the neighborhood. Most of our weekends and family moments consisted of playtime. There were times when we would wait until it was dark outside, turn off all the lights, close all the shades making the inside of our apartment as dark as possible while the only shadows we saw were created by the light that crept through the sides of the shades reflecting from the streetlights as we prepared to play hide-n-go-seek. On the occasions when they would invite friends over to join us it was not unusual for someone to start a food-fight or a water-gun fight. I enjoyed this playtime because it gave me an opportunity to know and mingle with my children's friends. Strangely enough, although I played with them, they never failed to respect me for the position that I held as an adult and a mother.

I showed up three months after my arrival to New York at the biggest and most prestigious medical center ready to begin working. I was well aware that people were betting upon my failure and hoping I would eventually end up on welfare and I was delighted to know that I was closer to proving them wrong than they could ever imagine. I was employed into a department, which at the time was in extreme need for a filing clerk. There were boxes, piles, bundles and stacks of paperwork all over the office. Although this was not my major position description, I along with the other new employee volunteered, with the approval of overtime to straighten out this mess. Melinda and I spent a few hours after work as well as weekends dedicating every spare moment to filing. Carolyn, the supervisor was the type of person who needed to know exactly what everybody was doing at every given moment of the day; therefore she would remain after work hours and come in on the weekends to watch and monitor our progress.

This monitoring went on for approximately two months until Carolyn decided that she couldn't continue spending all of her spare time at the office, therefore she asked a friend from another department to take over these duties. Norah was now acting as supervisor in Carolyn's absence. Norah, being hyper in character did not enjoy the idea of idly sitting around for hours, therefore she decided to take a box and assist with the process. While going through the boxes, Norah decided that much of the paperwork was unnecessary and duplicated. Being new to the organization, I was very much unaware of the importance of any of the forms or the paperwork. I was simply filing according to name, social security number and category as I had been originally instructed. Norah began sorting through the paperwork and discarding what she felt was unnecessary. I followed her instructions completely including the instruction to keep this secret amongst the three of us.

Monday morning brought a harsh reality when word had gotten around that some paperwork had been illegally discarded. It seems that one of the other workers in the office had previously had an upsetting encounter with Norah and this was the perfect weapon that she needed to establish a case against her. Not only did this become an embarrassment within the office but gossip of this incident quickly spread throughout the entire medical center. Carolyn was livid. On Tuesday morning I was pulled away from my daily activities, taken to a location where no one was present except Carolyn and myself, questioned again and again regarding what type of paperwork was involved. Carolyn scrunched up her face, stomped her feet, made a fist and hit the file cabinet while standing within inches of my face. I wanted to beat the hell out of her, but I knew that it would be my word against hers and I was determined at this point that I was not going down without a fight. She became even more annoyed as I calmly told her that I did nothing more than follow the instructions of the supervisor that she chose to place in charge. Although I was just as furious as she was she was in control, however I was determined that I was not going to back down from her either. I had two children that were depending upon me therefore she was surely in for a fight.

The next few weeks were filled with hostility between Carolyn and me. The female that instigated the whole situation was constantly snickering and whispering because she had gotten her satisfaction against Norah not caring who else's reputation was involved. Employees from other departments insisted upon knowing if their personal information was incorrectly discard. I was then informed that since I had not yet passed probation that my employment and the other new employee's employment would be instantly terminated, however Norah was not going to be terminated because she had so many years on the job that it would not be proper to terminate her. I then began to retaliate by writing letters to the hospital chairman, president, vice-president and anyone else that I thought would listen. I demanded to know how I could be terminated for following the order of a supervisor. Several days went by and the tension grew thick within the office. The insults, the snickering and the rudeness that I endured were almost unbearable. I thought about quitting, but my pride would not let me go down like that. Several meetings were held one after another until the final meeting, which consisted of Carolyn, Norah, the head manager and me. I was instructed to sit quietly with my head down and look sorry for what I had done, anything which needed to be said, would be said by Carolyn. However, the

Department Manager looked directly at me and requested to know exactly what had occurred. Grateful that he'd ask, through my anger I blurted out every detail just as it had occurred not caring what Carolyn or Norah thought of my actions. Once again, I was in trouble with Carolyn and from the look on her face I knew that she was fishing for a chance to punish me severely. As the meeting was ending the department manager informed me that I would be contacted regarding a decision upon my employment or termination from the company. It wasn't long before Carolyn informed me that Melinda did not pass her probationary period, but I did. This led to a long and bitter relationship between Carolyn and me. Carolyn informed me that she did not approve of this decision and that she would see to it that I never advance, transfer or promote from that department for as long as I was employed with the company. She did everything in her power to force me to quit, but she soon found out that her advancements towards me were not going to be as easy as she thought. At this time I was not only receiving verbal threats from her, but also from her family members as well. One day while on my way home her son who towered over me in height approached me and threatened that if I gave his mother any more problems he would do bodily harm to me. Her sisters would visit the office and accidentally bump into me with a threatening smile or gesture. I was determined to stand my grounds and no threat would cause me to move from this position.

Approximately one year later Barbara was employed into the department as a summer student during her junior year of high school. I later found out that Barbara was the girlfriend of Carolyn's nephew. Barbara was a well-dressed, Well-spoken young woman who carried a professional attitude at all times. She and I became friends much to Carolyn's objection. Although Barbara had heard about the previous incidents between Carolyn and me, she vowed to remain a neutral partner. Barbara did what she was hired to do for the summer and in September terminated to continue her schooling. There were numerous situations, which occurred during the following year that I either ignored or dealt with the best way I knew how. These situations included the day Carolyn's daughter and Niece entered the office during a time that Carolyn was away in a meeting, her daughter removed Carolyn's purse from the drawer, removed the bankcard and cash from her wallet while her niece stood guard at the door. I looked around and realized that I was the only one in the office with these two young ladies and was cautious to believe that this was another set-up. When they left, I picked up the phone and placed a call into the office of the department manager explaining what had just occurred. I was not going to jail for theft!

It seemed that the year passed quickly and soon, Barbara was back. After high school graduation, she was delighted to know that she had a permanent position within the department. She did not know that she was being used as a plot against me and neither did she know was that I was not that easy to deal with. The anger that had built up inside of me at this point was atrocious. The local newspapers began carrying stories about office workers who walked into their places of employment with guns and just shot up the place; Boy, did that sound like a good idea to me right now. If only I had a gun. The months went on and the abuse continued. The plots against me took many winding twists and failed at every end. I was passed up for promotions, denied transfers, given unfair ratings on employment references, mislead in trainings and miscalculated upon accruals for time off.

I had been employed now for approximately nine years when Laura transferred from the payroll office. Laura knew nothing regarding the type of work that was required within the department and being the senior personnel I took on the task of training her just as I had done many times before with other new employees. Laura and I became acquaintances as I taught her what the job required. A few months later her attitude towards me became very strange. The day had come to an end and everybody was taking that last trip to the bathroom just before packing to go home. The ladies room was a public bathroom with five stalls and four wash sinks. Laura and I usually took that trip together just as friends usually do. This particular day, when I mentioned that I was going to the bathroom, Laura blurted out in a loud voice, "go ahead, I'll wait until you come back and them I'll go". Excuse me, I said as I turned to face her. "What do you think I'm gonna do rape you? You don't have anything that I want, trust me!" I was fuming, not because she didn't take the trip with me but because I smelled another snake about to creep up. I realized that that statement was not for me but something under-handed, devious and dirty was brewing again and Laura had given me fair warning.

As I slept I began envisioning signs of warnings telling me that a friend was about to betray me. Not knowing why, I had this feeling deep within my guts alerting me to clean up my working area. Therefore, I removed all personal items including family pictures, food, comb and brushes. Several days later Laura secretly slipped a number into my hands. Go talk to this doctor she advised as she walked away. I saw the seriousness in her eyes and realized that the number was not for a medical doctor, but a doctor of supernatural sciences.

NEVER FORGIVE, NEVER FORGET

It was LaChelle's sixteenth birthday. Party plans were already in progress, invitations had been passed out and security measures were settled. The cake was ordered and the meal was planned the only thing left to do was blow up the balloons and decorate the apartment. One room was emptied of all furniture so that it could be used as a dance floor and the neighbors were alerted of the beginning and ending times. LaChelle had recently broken up with her boyfriend and was expecting a new friend as the guest of honor. Her ex-boyfriend lived two floors below and security was alerted that he was not invited to this party. LaChelle had been given instructions to remain inside the apartment for the entire evening. It wasn't long before the entire apartment was overflowing with teenage energy. As people arrived LaChelle introduced me to the friends that I was not familiar with which included a very polite, very quiet young man named Marcus. For most of the evening he stood back and observed the happenings. The night went very smoothly and LaChelle woke up the next day very much satisfied.

A year later I unexpectedly arrived home early from work to find Marcus in LaChelle's bedroom. Regardless to how I felt or dealt with the situation, this did not prevent me from coming home again and again with the same encounter. Once again I let Marcus and LaChelle know that this was not acceptable behavior and that I did not appreciate my home being disrespected in this way; a few months later I overheard the announcement of LaChelle's pregnancy, unfortunately, this was after the abortion. During her telephone conversations she was expressing to her friend how Marcus had insisted that she abort because he was not going to support the child because he was too young to be a dad, yet she ended the conversation expressing his never-ending love for her. I decided to address LaChelle and Marcus upon their actions. I explained to both of them that an abortion was not an acceptable method of birth control and that I was not going to allow LaChelle to cut up her body to satisfy him. I made it clear that this would never happen again. While LaChelle and Marcus continued their adventures whenever they found the time, space and accessibility to do so school became second concern for both of them and my home became the user-friendly party spot.

Three months later LaChelle announced that she was pregnant again. I made it clear to inform her that nine months from that date she would be a mother if God saw fit to bring this pregnancy to a conclusion. When LaChelle announced this decision to Marcus, he instantly insisted that regardless to what I say, she was going to have an abortion. It was at that moment that she developed enough courage to stand up to him and informed him that she will endure this pregnancy to full term. Marcus became excessively angry and began accusing her of purposefully ruining his life. A few days later he announced to her that she was forbidden to show her face at his home because his father was furious about her decision and threatened to physically hurt her if she came over. He continued by telling her how he has no place to live because his father threw him out of the house because of this situation. He called her all types of sluts, whores, and home wreckers and told her that the baby was not his and that he was not going to support any child that he did not produce. This behavior went on for months.

LaChelle's was in her sixth month of pregnancy when she decided that she needed to face Marcus's father herself. Mr. Harris' threats of physical violence for the sake of protecting his son's innocence were no longer a threat to LaChelle. Annoyance had forced her to the point where she jumped into a taxi and headed for Marcus's house. As boldness and anger stirred within her, she was determined that she was going to stand before his father eye to eye. Much to her surprise, when Mr. Harris opened the door and peered down upon this obviously pregnant young girl, he was flabbergasted. The shock of knowing that he was about to become a grandfather brought on great bewilderment within the Harris household. It was obvious to LaChelle that this was the first time that Mr. Harris had become aware of this situation. Confusion began to enrage within her as she thought about the threats that Marcus had been passing to her from his father. Lies, they were all lies.

This angered Marcus even more as he tried to convince his father, his friends and the rest of his family that this was definitely not his child because he was not sexually involved with this girl and he wanted nothing to do with her or that kid. According to Marcus, LaChelle was crazy. She was stalking him with the intentions of ruining his life. She was demanding to have a relationship with him and when he refused to submit, she went to the measures of trying to trap him with a pregnancy that he had no involvements with. He told stories about how LaChelle was a hot headed, sexually loose girl who was promiscuous with every boy in school.

When he realized that his lies was not convincing enough, Marcus then decided that there was another way to avoid this entire situation; therefore he voluntarily signed himself into the United States Navy and suddenly disappeared. LaChelle had no idea where he was stationed and after several months she stopped inquiring about him. Months passed with no contact between LaChelle and Marcus. LaChelle continued her education and walked across the stage to collect her high school diploma the following June.

Regardless of what the situation was, reality had Mr. Harris so overwhelmed and knowing that he was about to be a grandfather forced him to keep his son updated with the progression of the pregnancy. Marcus was the only connection that Mr. Harris had for a relationship with his first grandchild and Mr. Harris was not going to walk away from this child without knowing the truth. Marcus failed over and over again trying to find someone to see it from his perspective and the resentment keeps turning over and over in his mind. Why didn't LaChelle get an abortion? Had she just gone through with an abortion this whole situation could have been avoided; so what, she just had an abortion for him three months previous, that's no reason why she could get another one and save his reputation. The embarrassment was wearing him down. All the other girls got an abortion, why couldn't she. Why is she so persistent to have this darn child anyway? Not realizing that his past has too much of a stronghold on him, Marcus settled into the Navy in an attempt for a new beginning, but in his mind there was something that he just couldn't shake or break away from because dear old dad keeps bringing this up-coming event back to his memory.

The news of the birth was devastating, although no one seemed to feel that way except Marcus, and to make it even more overwhelming, it had to be a boy. Oh, my God, Junior! The following day Mr. Harris visited the hospital to meet his first-born grandson. He studied every inch of the baby's body trying to find identifying features or marks that either connected or disconnected the child to his son. He honestly wanted to be the proud grandfather, but he was contemplating with the theory of his son's story this girl was promiscuous and the child could belong to any number of people. Little did he know, time would tell all!

Several months had passed and LaChelle had begun reorganizing her life, seeking employment, registering for school and interviewing babysitters. The only contact that LaChelle had with Marcus was receiving word through his father that Marcus was Okay and wanted to come meet his son. I was furious, his son? Now he wants to acknowledge that he has a son? What makes him think he has that right? Finally, Lo and behold the day came that Marcus decided to pick up the phone and give LaChelle a call. He explained how the Navy keeps him extremely busy and he's always underway which he continued to explain that that means that the ship was constantly out to sea. He explains that the military life is so demanding that he never has much time for himself anymore. Being an Army brat, LaChelle began comparing what he was saying to the lifestyle that she knew; but of course according to Marcus the Navy is much busier than the Army. He promises her that he will be home soon to visit and he will stop by to meet his new son. By now the little respect that I tried to have for him has dwindled drastically.

Just as Marcus promised the day had come to meet his son. I watched in disgust as he went through the examination process of touching his hair, turning his hands over again and again and finally taking the socks off to examine his feet. I realized that he was trying to find signs of familiarity, but it didn't matter to me whether he accepted this child or not, this was my grandchild and that was the only fact. Although there was no doubt in LaChelle's mind who the father was, Marcus continued looking for that small miracle which would separate him from this situation permanently. During this meeting the only information Marcus would reveal regarding his location was that he was stationed in Norfolk, Virginia.

The baby was nine months old when he began to show signs of breathing struggles. LaChelle spent hours in the Emergency Room and finally they decided to admit him. Like usual, LaChelle contacted Marcus's father in an effort to contact Marcus. Marcus Junior spent several nights in the hospital receiving breathing treatments. The doctor explained that the baby had a rare breathing disorder that they could not place a name to, but because it's compatible to asthma, they're treating it in the same manner. A few days later LaChelle was given a machine, some medication and instructions to assist the baby with breathing exercises and Marcus Junior was released. The next day I received a phone call from Mr. Harris instructing me upon an over-the-counter treatment which would definitely cure this breathing condition. Out of desperation I purchased the product and just as he'd predicted, upon the next visit to the doctor, there was no sign of a breathing condition in Marcus Junior. During the next conversation that I had with Mr. Harris I questioned how he knew what to do to cure the problems and he informed me that Marcus was born with the same breathing condition. I then realized that this incident is what convinced Mr. Harris that Marcus Junior was definitely his grandson and it was at this moment that they officially accepted the baby into their family.

The older Marcus Junior became, the more Marcus hated LaChelle for even allowing this pregnancy to be carried to full term. Marcus hated the mere idea that this little creature was connected to him in any sort of way. He couldn't face the fact that LaChelle actually attached "junior" to the end of his name. He was determined that some how, no matter how long it took, he was going to get her back for causing him such an embarrassment, he wanted her to experience the feelings of having your dreams crumbled right in the palms of your hand. He felt stuck for life, bonded by the birth of a child that was never agreed upon. He wanted desperately to erase this portion of his life, but he did not know how. He was in bondage. He never realized how one mistake could change a person's life so drastically. It's like a nightmare that can't go away; and the bad part about it all is that she's still in love with him. Marcus felt that his dad was not helping by telling him that he should pay child support for this child. Those words were like a razor sharp knife that went straight through him, slicing him into millions of pieces each time. It felt as if he was in a fight with Edward Scissor-hands, knives rotating, swinging and striking in your direction with calculated force.

The hatred became too much to handle as Marcus tried to cope. He tried to be proud of this child and even tried to love his baby's mother, but the initial embarrassment kept weighing him down. Nobody seemed to understand that his remaining hope of a successful future has now been diminished to a blurred question mark. Marcus wanted nothing more than to make his dad proud of him, but can he find a way to turn this mistake into something that could once again make his dad proud to call him son? Is it possible to have hatred embedded so deeply within your soul that it creates a shadow over your entire ability to function from day to day? What experiences can life throw your way that forces you into a position which makes you unable to move ahead because there is something so strongly pulling you into the center of its core that it seems like your whole world is surrounded by thick, hard mass that cannot possible be penetrated. How can you bail out when you're drowning in hurt and embarrassed so deeply cutting into your soul that you feel as if even the love of God cannot unravel these emotions? How can Marcus now tell his dad that he's an average child, that he's done what his dad has deemed to be "ghetto-like" or "project mentality". That he perhaps was not going to college because he now has a bigger responsibility to handle. What type of image was this going to set before the Ladies? This would surely shatter his image of being the "Mack", "A woman's man", "Every woman's sexual desire". His life was not supposed to consist of this kind of drama.

THE FIRST CHRISTMAS

Christmas was LaChelle's favorite holiday. There was something about the season that seemed to bring out the little girl that lingered within her. The twinkling of colorful lights shone in the windows of the apartments throughout the neighborhood, jolly music possessed every radio station and peace took control of people as they wandered from store to store, aisle to aisle trying to purchase that perfect gift for that special somebody in their lives and most of all the smell of real pine gave the house a fresh, clean smell of nature in the middle of a winter wonderland. While many of the presents still lied open beneath the tree, there was still a few yet waiting to be presented to friends and family that hasn't yet come to claim them. LaChelle had saved an extensive amount of money that she'd collected from the tips she'd received from her job as a waitress at Applebee's to buy Marcus the Timberland boots that he repeatedly made mentions of. Just two months ago she'd bought him the Durangos that he'd wanted for his birthday to match his new leather coat. It was about 6:00 in the evening when he arrived. Soon as he settled himself on the sofa she excitedly reached beneath the tree and handed him the neatly wrapped box with the red bow along with a box labeled "To Daddy from Marcus". In return he presented her with a small box, which enclosed a nativity statute of Mary, Joseph and baby Jesus along with an outfit for the baby. LaChelle then reached over and kissed him on the cheek; Thank You she said as she rose from the sofa and placed her gifts on the dining room table. She seemed vaguely disappointed, but I dare not ask why as he offered her a subtle smile curled to one side of his mouth as he returned the "Thank You". While she sat patiently waiting, bursting with anticipation waiting to capture his expression as he viewed the contents inside his present, instead he placed the unopened gifts on the sofa next to him then began to make small conversation about the baby's progressions. LaChelle entertained his chitchat for a short while before asking him why he wasn't opening the gifts. Oh, I will, he replied as he pretended to focus his entire attention on the baby. She began to look very annoyed as he once again proceeded to examine the baby for any sign of comparison wishing that he could disconnect himself from this child and I knew that Chelle was biting her tongue about the subject.

Another subtle smile, another idle conversation, another examination and then he were ready to go. Why aren't you opening your presents she inquired once again; Oh yea, he replied then picked up the smaller gift and quickly opened the framed picture of the baby. Cute, he replied and placed it back on the sofa. Then he opened the large box. O.K. he replied sounding a little more excited, these are nice. How much did they cost? I like the color. Light blue, huh, what do you think I can wear with these, oh yea, I have my blue stripped sweater that I could wear with my jeans. He looked them over for a few more minutes, "well I guess I better be getting out of here" he replied as he tucked the box under his arms and proceeded towards the door. Aren't you going to take your other gift with you she asked? I'll be back for it he replied as he gave her a quick kiss, took another glimpse of the baby in her arms and walked out the door.

LaChelle looked over at me as I was looking back at her. We had a way of conversing with body language and through hers I recognized total disappointment. She knew exactly what I was thinking as she placed the baby on the bed, picked up the gift, stuck the bow on the corner and placed it back under the tree. I knew that I wasn't satisfied with these visits and I wanted my daughter to be happy, but the formation of this relationship was really shaking my nerves. It seemed that while LaChelle was pouring her heart out to him, he was treating her as if he was much too good for her and she should be appreciative just to know someone of his character. It reminded me very much of the relationship that I had with my ex-husband. I slightly hinted my point to her, but not wanting to put a damper on our relationship. I prayed that this relationship was just a passing phase and that Chelle would find someone who respected her. The majority of contact between her and Marcus consisted of telephone conversations and every now and then she would pack up the baby and travel to Virginia for a weekend visit.

AN UNEXPECTED VISIT

It was late night and LaChelle was busy entertaining herself with her favorite pass-time, talking on the telephone, singing to the radio and dancing around her room. I was beginning to believe that the telephone receiver was permanently attached to her right ear and at times it seemed painful to watch how she had perfected the art of holding it between her ear and shoulder blade for hours at a time. I couldn't imagine holding my neck in that position that long without getting a cramp, but it never seemed to bother her at all. Her bedroom was a complete and total mess, like always. Marcus Junior was sleeping on the bed next to her. All I could hear was the sound of passing cars and people on the streets below and the loud conversation that Chelle was carrying on with whoever was on the other end of the receiver. The noise didn't seem to bother Marcus Junior at all. He seemed to be in such a peaceful slumber.

I had just finished cleaning the kitchen and I was bored. Needing to create a way to grasp her attention, I eased up to her bedroom door and peeked between the cracks of the doorframe to view her whereabouts. Just as I had imagined, she was now resting against the headboard and the telephone receiver resting on her left shoulder, which freed her hands to polish her toenails. I grinned to myself knowing that I was up to absolutely no-good as I adjusted my face to portray a serious expression. I walked into her bedroom, removed a piece of paper from her dresser and quickly exited, knowing that she would chase me. Hold on, she abruptly spoke into the receiver as she jumped from the bed and ran behind me through the living room, the dining room and into my bedroom. Ma, what was that she beckoned in the haste. The apartment was fairly small so there wasn't much room for dodging the attack that I had instigated. I tried to jump across my bed to the other side when she grabbed my shirt from behind and pulled me closer to her as she tried to pry my fist open to view the contents inside. I held on tight but the hysterical laughter caused my body to lose strength. Falling to the floor, we rolled over and over across the carpet as she struggled again and again to open my fist. She knew that tickling me was no competition; therefore we struggled until I finally gave up and opened my hand. She gave me an annoying look and struggled to get back on her feet as she realized that I was holding a grocery receipt. She left me there laughing as she rolled her eyes, sucked her teeth and went back into her room. Hello, I heard her speak into the telephone; my mother's acting crazy again. At this time I was standing in her doorway looking around the room as if I was about snatch something else. Ma, she yelled as she sprung up from the bed, walked over to me, spun me around and shoved me from the doorway.

Just as she was closing the door, the doorbell rang. We both looked at each other in confusion. LaChelle shrugged her shoulders in awe as I headed towards the intercom to investigate the call. "Who is it", I inquired into the box. Marcus was the reply. LaChelle's mouth dropped opened in amazement. I have to go; she spoke into the receiver as she hasted to clean up her bedroom a bit. She kicked shoes under the bed, shoved clothes into the closet and closed the closet door. She threw the bedspread across the bed and toys into the baby's crib. She slightly closed the bedroom door behind her as she tiptoed quickly towards the front door. Hello she said with a wide grin as he invited him in. I didn't know you were coming, what are you doing here she asked as he brushed pass her with a kiss on the cheek and a curious eye that scanned the apartment. Hello Ms. Williams he said while walking towards the living room. Hello Marcus, I replied as I trailed behind them. Do you realize what time it is? Yes, he apologized. I know it's late, but I just got in town and I wanted to see the baby before I go home. The baby's sleeping I replied and we were about to go to bed, you couldn't wait until morning to see the baby? Well, Marcus explained, I'm only going to be here only for a short while and tomorrow I will be doing a lot of running around for my dad and I wanted to make sure I see him before I leave. I looked at LaChelle, rolled my eyes and walked back into my bedroom. There was something about his demeanor that puzzled me, so I positioned myself so that I could listen and watch hoping to find out what his real intentions were. Chelle began by telling him how much she'd missed him. She then began to update him upon all the new things that the baby was doing. He listened, but his reply let me know that he was not at all interested in anything that she was saying to him. My curiosity broadened as he motioned towards the bathroom, knowing that he had to pass her bedroom. I followed from a distance so that I could get a glimpse of his actions just as he jokingly pushed open the door to view the entire room. He nodded his head in approval as he gave her a slight smile and went into the bathroom. I walked into the kitchen disgusted and debating whether or not I wanted to make a comment regarding his examination and how he casually inched his way into her bedroom for a closer look. I made another comment to let him know that I was not satisfied with his surprise appearance. He sat on her bed and began a casual conversation as if he didn't hear anything that I had just said. His back was towards the door and LaChelle was facing him. As LaChelle glared up at me she realized that I was becoming very annoyed and I knew that she was trying to find a nice way to ask him to leave, so I decided to let her handle the situation. I was standing in the doorway as he lifted the corner of her bedspread and began scolding her regarding the conditions of her bedroom. With a stern voice I said, Marcus I have to go to work tomorrow, therefore you need to leave now. You can come back tomorrow at a decent time if you choose to do so, but right now you have to go. From the look on my face LaChelle knew that I was fed up with the defiance and I was not in a position where I was willing to compromise. She followed as he headed towards the door. What the heck did he want? I asked as the door closed behind him. He just wanted to say hello and let me know that he was here she replied as she turned and walked back towards her bedroom. I knew that she really didn't believe him and I knew that his visit was not to check on the welfare of the baby at all.

This was the beginning of a long string of unexpected visits from Virginia to New York and it was this nature of visits that forced the conclusion of my previous judgment that he was extremely sneaky, audacious and arrogant. I did not like the uncomfortable feelings that he was forcing me to experience in my own home. My inner conscience was alerting me that he was up to something. Perhaps he was trying to catch her in an uncompromising situation, probably sexually involved with another guy and his aim was to place me in a position of saying that I was allowing ungodly acts to happen within my household. I don't know what made him think he had a right to force me to feel guilty for any decision that I made in my home and I really didn't care whether he liked me or not I had no reason to explain any actions or decisions to him or anyone else. I was annoyed with the mere fact that he insisted upon mentally imprisoning us with the idea that he might show up at any time as if he was some kind of threat. The idea of this person who didn't contribute to the rent payment, bill payment or support of LaChelle nor the baby, being half my age had the audacity to believe that he had some type of control over my choices for the purpose of controlling the child that I single-handedly raised was annoying the hell out of me. I was angry at the idea that he obvious deemed her as his personal property, taking away her entire identity as a free human being. My mind automatically began to remember the times that I came home from work early finding him in my daughter's bed. Even then, I tried to explain to Chelle that any man that would disrespect your home in that manner would never respect you as a person. I couldn't help but wonder what influence he had on her that would force her to keep her mouth shut and permit these things to go on although it was more than obvious that this person was bold and extremely controlling.

When I expressed my annoyance of his antagonism, LaChelle instantly protected him by trying to convince me that I was over-reacting and that things were not what I was making them out to be. She also tried to convert me by explaining that he's not the person that I described him to be, but my mind was settled. Regardless to how much she tried to persuade me that he's really a nice person and pleaded with me to give him another chance my mind was settled. I saw what I saw and trusting in that previous impression, I had no intention of changing my mind. My motherly instincts were telling me that there was something about this guy that just wasn't right. This guy was up to something beyond measure, something sneaky and absolutely no-good. I couldn't connect to what his intentions were, but I knew that her future was going to be violent. You just don't like him because he's Jamaican she replied. Perhaps she was right because in my mind I imagined her being his personal prisoner. I saw abuse and extensive mistreatment beyond measure and each time I tried to make her understand she protected him even more. I remember when my mother once said sometimes you have to let a person hit a brick wall in order for them to realize what you are trying to tell them. I didn't want my daughter to hit that brick wall, but I knew somehow she was going to continue running into it at full force. I realized that, like many young women her age, she had the dream of bring her family together in holy matrimony in hopes that her son could have a close relationship with his dad, a relationship that she wished she could have had with hers. I couldn't make her understand that those actions were not in her control and somehow I got the feeling that she understood what I was saying, but she didn't want to accept it. Marcus didn't seem to have the same dream. He wanted to let her know that since she dragged him into her life, she had to deal with whatever he had to offer. I prayed that God would reveal a sign to Chelle that would change her course of direction before she'd experience any of his vindictiveness, but it seemed that she'd had her mind made up. She was willing to give it a try.

Marcus was creating a wedge on the close relationship that I once had with my daughter and I was insistent upon holding onto the little admiration that we had left for each other. I knew that Chelle was going to need me in the future and I was determined that Marcus was not going to force us apart.

LIES, LIES AND ALIBIES

I couldn't help but notice the changes in LaChelle's character since she and Marcus has resolved the differences in their relationship and sometimes it angers me to see how much she would deny herself for the purpose of fulfilling his satisfactions. It was New Year's Eve when I dropped off LaChelle and the baby at the Greyhound bus station. The trip to Virginia would take approximately eight hours and there was only one seat remaining on the bus. This meant that LaChelle would hold the baby on her lap for the entire trip. Marcus Junior was a very active child and very solid in weight so trying to detain him in one position for that length of time was definitely going to be a challenge, but Chelle was determined to arrive in Virginia just in time to tip the clock and share the moment with Marcus when 2001 rang in.

LaChelle and I were accustomed to conversing daily and although I hadn't spoken to her in two days, I wasn't too worried about it because certainly she would call eventually to update me upon her daily adventures. We somehow must have been on the same brain waves because just then the phone rang. Normally her excitement of Virginia consisted of the beauty of the state and the never-ending attractions of oceans, boats and clear blue skies that you just don't get in New York anymore but this phone call was very unusual. It must have been the sound of the ring that kicked in my mother instinct of concern. Mom, she whispered, guess what? Her voice was anxious, but not sad, therefore I wasn't expecting to hear any bad news, neither could I understand why she was whispering, but I played along with the scenario. What, I replied anxiously waiting to hear what her next discovery, evening with her friends or baby story was. "Guess what me and Marcus just did", she whispered into the receiver and with a snicker she blurted out "we just went down to City Hall and got married". My mouth fell open as my mind began to race along with my imagination trying to recreate a picture of the whole scene. Yea, right! I replied in disbelief. Actually I was testing the grounds to get a feel of whether or not she was serious. It was not abnormal for LaChelle to tease around with me, telling me ridiculous stories just to catch my reaction. I'm serious Mom she said, we did. I suddenly felt myself getting a little annoyed at this report as I gathered my words to reply. First of all I replied with a very annoyed voice, why are you whispering? I wanted her to know that I didn't appreciate this joke as I completed the question with "and what in the hell was the big rush"? Mom, she replied I know you're angry and I will give you details when I get back to New York. I'm whispering because Marcus doesn't want anyone to know about it yet. He went to get something from the car, so I wanted to call you real quick, but he's about to come in so I have to go. I'll talk with you later, bye mom she said and hastily hung up the telephone. Standing there still in amazement with the receiver in my hand I was trying to figure out why would she go and do something like this. This was very much out of character for her. I could never have imagined she would go and do something like this without at least hinting me first. In my opinion, the relationship between her and Marcus still had a whole lot of kinks that needed to be worked out. Yes they had a baby together, but as far as I could see, there were no sign of love within that relationship whatsoever. The confusion in my mind is trying to figure out what was the reasoning behind this dramatic scuttle. There had better be a darn good reason, I mean something had better be about to explode.

Sunday was soon approaching and I have to be at the Am track station at least by 11:30 P.M. to pick up LaChelle and the baby. I can't wait to acquire details of this venture. My mind was racing, my heart was pumping and my blood pressure was about to reach the roof. Has she lost her doggone mind? There are so many questions going through my mind right now that I'm having problems focusing on a single thought. Time just was not moving fast enough for me. It seems that I'm hitting every single red light from the Bronx to Manhattan, everybody suddenly needs to cross the street and of course there are no available meters to park the car. LaChelle was due to arrive at midnight, and just when I was beginning to think that nothing else could possibly go wrong the overhead pager announced that the train was going to be late. There were no attendants available who could tell me if she had even boarded the train. This wouldn't be the first time that she missed the schedule, perhaps Marcus decided at the last moment that he had something more important to do than drive her to the station, but I'm sitting out here on 34th street in Manhattan all alone waiting. I'm an open target for muggers, rapist, con artist and thugs who are always lurking in the shadows for those who simply look vulnerable. After wandering around about an hour I once again tried to obtain information on the arrival time of her train. The arrival time that was passing across the information board has already passed and the attendants on duty didn't seem to have any updates. I'd tried to reach Marcus's cell phone several times and only received his voice mail. I'd already left several messages and did not receive a call back. Unsure of what to do without looking as if I were lost or walking in circles I decided that the safest thing to do was to drive back to the Bronx in hopes that she or Marcus would call my cell phone so that I could make a return trip. I hated to have to leave her in Grand Central Station alone with a baby knowing that she would be even more vulnerable than I was.

There was no category for my anger level now. We have had these discussions time and time again and she knows that when she takes these trips she needs to get an early return train not only because I have to go to work the next day, but for safety if nothing else. When I reached home the first thing I did was check the answering machine to see if she or Marcus had left me a message. The light was not blinking which meant, no messages. Now I don't know if I'm worried or irritated to no end, but what I do know is that I want to scream to the top of my voice just for the purposes of letting off steam. I couldn't help but question the thought in my mind of what kind of husband would place his family in such a life-threatening situation. Of course there was no way I could go to sleep now. My adrenaline was flowing faster than an exploding volcano. The local train station was a three block walk up the hill and the neighborhood in which I grew up has degraded so radically in the past few years that I was afraid to be walking alone at this time of the night, but I had a child out there and a grandchild that possibly might need my help, therefore nothing was going to keep me behind these walls until I know that they are safe. Brutes were prowling the neighborhood in aspiration of whatever dilemma they could get into and whomever they could possibly detain for their own selfish pleasures. In my opinion this was a very selfish, self-centered and unconcerned action and once again I've promised myself that I would never be caught in this position again. It annoyed me to think that LaChelle would put someone else above her own demeanor and place herself in this type of situation to satisfy a man that has shown very little concern for her welfare since the relationship began. In case no one has noticed, I've never really cared for this relationship and I have no need to give a hoot if it succeeds, but that haven't stopped me from worrying. On my way to the train station a man in a silver Maxima pulled up beside me and gestured me to get into the car. I ignored his aggressiveness and kept walking pretending to not hear his command until he quickly parked the car and attempted to pursue in my direction. I ran the remaining two blocks to the station and up the stairs where the night attendant sat in the token booth. As I stood nervously waiting for the train to pull into the station I began a conversation with the attendant mentioning to her how the man was chasing me. Oh, is that all she said, that goes on all the time around here, you're lucky that's all he did. I was very puzzled by her unconcern. When I was growing up in this neighborhood it was never like this. I remember when I used to walk the streets all alone at night and never worried about being mugged, raped or kidnapped or perhaps I was too young to realize the dangers of it all, but as far as I could remember these streets were never this bad. These were usually the kind of stories you hear about from the South Bronx. She began to explain to me how White Plains Road had became a drug paradise about two years ago and how the thugs now own the boulevard when the sun goes down.

The train pulled up and a few people got off, but no Chelle. I tried to keep in step with the two people that were walking in the direction that I needed to go to get back home. I was even more afraid now knowing that LaChelle was out there somewhere with a baby, a stroller and three overnight bags trying to get home. I paced the floor back and forth from the window to the door and from room to room and window to window. By now I don't know if I want to be angry or scared. Then I heard the familiar sound of a baby crying. I certainly knew the sound of that particular cry and knew that it was Marcus Junior I ran downstairs and into the direction of the cry to help her up with all the things that she was carrying. I was so happy to know that she was safe that I almost forgot how angry I was, besides I have to go to work soon, so I'll just take this time to get in a few hours of sleep. I'll go in depth with her on this subject later. The last thing I noticed was LaChelle scrambling through the refrigerator for something to eat and something to feed the baby. LaChelle woke me up a few hours later by shaking me on the shoulder asking to borrow a few dollars until payday. As tired as I was I had to speak out, didn't you just leave Marcus, I blurted; again he sent you home with no money. What in the hell do you go see him for, he's a waste. I knew that she was going to give me the "he didn't have any money" story that I was so tired of hearing; he never seems to have any money for her or the baby. It seems that he's the only one that works constantly and never gets paid.

LaChelle really had no intention of keeping the marriage a secret especially amongst family, but concluded by asking them not to mention this in the presence of Marcus. She wore an engagement ring on her left hand, which she explained that Marcus wanted everybody think they were engaged. She carried a certain glow in her appearance revealing the fact that she was happy to know that she had finally brought her family together. This was obviously a very dear and touching moment in her life and in her book of dreams. At least she thought so. I was very much dissatisfied with this situation and the set-up. Something inside of me kept telling me that something was not right, that something underhanded was about to happen, but I could not figure out what it was. Marcus has finally drawn her into his world of lies. There were too many things that puzzled my mind about this situation, but LaChelle has already made up her mind that she was going to be the best wife that she could possibly be. In a conversation later, LaChelle explained to me that she did not want to struggle to raise her children as she had seen me do for so many years. When I brought my concerns to LaChelle, She assured me that she felt that she had done the right thing for her family. Well mom, LaChelle began explaining, Marcus is going underway for a few months and he wanted to be assured that in the event that anything should happen to him, junior and me would be taken care of. The reason why I'm wearing an engagement ring instead of a wedding band is because his grandmother wanted him to use her wedding ring when he got married and he hasn't gotten it from his dad yet. I wasn't buying it. It still made no sense to me. I didn't trust that scenario, but the damage has already been done. LaChelle had made her decision and it was obvious that she was sticking by it regardless to what I said.

During Marcus's next visit unaware that everybody knew about the marriage, he intentionally acted as if he and LaChelle were just friends. He kept to himself, did not mingle much with the rest of the family and just smiled and nodded every now and then when someone acknowledged his presence. And with this LaChelle pretended to be satisfied. Marcus had yet one more obstacle to cross. How was he going to break this news to his dad or anyone else in his family? He feared that his dad would, like always, tell him that he was just sinking deeper into more trouble. He did not want to hear how he had ruined his life he just didn't want to face the rejection. The thought of being hated by his family was incredibly overbearing so he chose to keep his family out of his immediate business. He just couldn't bear to hear how he'd failed again, so he had no other choice to live a lie even if he didn't want to. Marcus never sought shelter for his family or made arrangements for their relocation to Virginia, instead LaChelle continued her trips back and forth while she and Marcus Junior resided within the residence of our two-bedroom apartment in New York.

One day out of curiosity, Mr. Harris asked Marcus why LaChelle visited him so often. Marcus lied by telling his dad how she was insisting upon having a relationship therefore she was stalking him. Knowing that his dad disliked LaChelle already simply because he felt that she wasn't good enough for his expectations of his son, the lies did not help the in any sort of way. But Marcus couldn't bear telling the truth; therefore he will keep things this way until he could think of another way to pacify his father. Mr. Harris was under the impression that LaChelle was ruining his son's life by seeking a love affair that she so desperately wanted to force his son into. Marcus had led his dad to believing that LaChelle was forcing herself on him due to the fact that they had a child. Never could he bring himself to telling his dad that LaChelle was visiting so often because she was his wife.

It seemed that the more Marcus tried to do the right thing, the worst his life became. The relationship went from one white lie to a black lie, blue lie and red lie until Marcus became a pathological liar in all areas of his life. Lying was something that had become so naturally uncontrollable that lies would flow from his mouth even when he had no intentions of telling one.

THE LONG ROAD HOME

I was due to go on vacation at the end of that week. Everyone knew that I would be traveling to Georgia to attend Philip's graduation from boot camp. It was raining the morning that we were due to leave. I had a few things left to do in preparation for the trip and I still had to pick up the rental van. LaChelle, her two-months old son, my niece and Philip's girlfriend were all in the final stages of packing. I was the only driver, which wasn't unusual. I enjoyed long-distance driving and I had made these types of trips many times before. It was February and we were trying to get on the road early because the weather from state to state was so unpredictable. The weather station did not predict any snow for the next couple of days in New York and we were pretty confident that the weather would only get better as we go further south. I suddenly began feeling sick, my throat became very scratchy and uncomfortable. It felt as if I was developing the symptoms of a sore throat, so I grabbed the Tylenol, Listerine and throat lozenges and threw them into my purse and proceeded with my plans.

We were just passing the last exit on the New Jersey turnpike when the toll attendant warned us that the weather station had just predicted a major snowstorm heading our way. She alerted us to be careful as she handed me the change. By the time we got to Maryland, the snow was so thick that driving and visibility had become extremely difficult. We continued to drive hoping to get as close to Georgia as possible before stopping in search of a hotel for the evening. After a while, there was no way of recognizing the roadway, ditches or exits. I found it wise to remain close behind a truck hoping that the truck driver was more familiar with the roadway than I. Suddenly the truck fell sideways into a ditch and everyone in the van was directing my driving, yet no one could see anything out of the front windshield. We were just crossing the boarder to North Carolina when the State Troopers began directing all cars off the highway. By this time my throat was so swollen that I could hardly swallow. Thank God that the exit led to a hotel. We pulled into something that looked like a parking spot and began gathering our suitcases. The hotel lobby was filled with people lying across the chairs, sofas, and floors and against the walls. LaChelle took care of the arrangements. She somehow convinced the clerk that I was in need of a doctor and that we had a small baby and the clerk assigned us to a room. The room was obviously in need of repairs therefore it was not well heated and the door held a gap of approximately two inches above the floor. We were grateful to be out of the weather. By shoving towels and blankets beneath the door, we survived the night. By the time the sun rose, we were starving. The streets were still covered with high levels of snow. The highways were not opened and we had no idea what we were going to do. We had run out of the little food that we traveled with and there were no stores or restaurants open. My condition was beginning to worsen and the clerk informed us that there were no hospitals in the area. I had no idea what type of sickness I had come down with, but I realized by now, that this was more than a sore throat.

Our cell phones had no air service and the hotel telephones were down. I knew that the family would be worried, but there were nothing that we could do. Several hours later the announcement was made that the highways had been opened with caution to drive carefully, so we attempted to begin traveling again. The van got stuck in snow banks so many times and so many times local people owning pick-up trucks equipped with snowplows rescued us. I had heard so many stories about white people and prejudice within the south that I became paranoid each time someone came to rescue us. Upon one occasion, a man directed me out of the driver's seat and drove the van to clearing. I realized then, that people are people and I thanked God for everyone that he sent my way that day. We were finally able to contact my ex-husband who instructed us to make our way to Fayetteville where we stayed at his home for the night. He was preparing to make the trip to Georgia also and we decided that it might be safer to travel together. By the time we reached Fayetteville, I couldn't eat, I couldn't talk and I couldn't swallow. The next day when the roads were clear and I wanted nothing more than to head back to New York. On the way, we made a quick stop in Norfolk, Virginia to drop off LaChelle and the baby where they'd prepared to spend a few days with Marcus. We reached New York late that evening. I dropped off the girls at home and headed for the emergency room where I was diagnosed with a severe case of strep throat. My strep levels were so high the doctors were amazed that I was still conscious. After hours of testing, I was given medication and released.

The next several months were followed with major sickness, my entire body had swollen up as if someone had blown me up like a balloon. I looked into the mirror and thought, O My God! I look like a blowfish. My feet were rounded, as a basketball so walking was impossible. LaChelle quit her job to remain home to care for me. She spent day after day carrying me around on her back to and from the bathroom. Those months consisted of one doctor appointment after another until one day I heard one doctor relate to another saying that my conditions were not normal and with my strep levels being so high, there was no way I should even be alive. Their major concern was my heart, which showed very little signs of stress. As soon as I reached a point where I could function on my own, I took Laura's advice and sought the help of a doctor of supernatural sciences.

Knowing nothing about this ceremony and having no idea what to expect I walked into the presence of this doctor. The chicken that was wandering around the room became very irate at my presence. I did not mention anything to this doctor about my previous sickness, as a matter of fact, I didn't tell him anything at all. The doctor did several rituals upon me then began telling me about my lifestyle including that my son was in the military. He informed me that there had been three spirits placed in my path, two of them were waiting to push me and one was there for protection. He then warned me not to stand at the edge of a train platform, at the edge of a street, top of steps, or near a window. The doctor predicted that I was about to do something within the next year, which was going to save my life, but in the interim, I was going to lose something very valuable to me. I had no idea what he was talking about and my only plans at that time were to change jobs. The next year consisted upon me losing one job after another. I was financially in trouble and didn't know where to turn or what to do. I finally received a call for a position that I had interviewed for at another local medical center. This job was paying extremely well and I was beginning to think I could finally settle down. After I had been in that position four months, I received a phone call from one of my co-workers at my previous employment. The caller spoke softly and quietly into the receiver saying, "they know where you are and they're coming for you". I recognized the voice and I knew exactly what the caller meant. She was speaking about Carolyn and her company of companions, but I had already passed probation on this job and received a creditable evaluation. My boss had assured me that I was doing a great job and she was very satisfied with my performance, therefore I didn't concern myself too much with that call.

The following Wednesday as I was packing to go home, my boss walked in and sat in the chair adjacent to my desk. With a casual tone of voice she asked, "How are things going"? Fine, I replied. Did you get into a disagreement with someone perhaps today or yesterday she asked. I thought for a second wondering why she'd ask such a question, No, I replied, Not as I could remember. She shook her head, gave a quick grin then said, "just asked" and walked out. I wasn't exactly puzzled because my imagination was leading me to remember the phone call. I didn't have a negative confrontation with anyone, but how could you explain this to someone who has known you only for a few months. The next day, Mid-afternoon, she came into the office and said that people have been complaining about my attitude. They said that you are very nasty and have cursed at them upon several occasions. Really? I replied did you receive these calls? No, she replied, the calls went into the office of the President and the response seeped down to me. You need to be very careful she replied and she walked out. By the end of the day Friday, I was given my last paycheck, told to take my belongings and leave. This time, there were no explanations. Although I knew exactly where these accusations were coming from, how could you explain to your boss that your previous employer is sabotaging you? This was a few months after the terrorist attack on New York, September 11, 2001. There were no jobs available except those that paid very little and required help with the searching of body parts at ground zero. Although I knew I was going to need every dime that I could get my hands on I was not about to go dig for body parts at minimum wage, therefore taking my daughter's advice I prepared to relocate to Virginia.

JUSTICE FOR A LADYBUG

A sudden lay-off was something that I had not anticipated and New York was still in an uproar. LaChelle greeted this opportunity with delight. Mom, she said, you've been looking for the perfect motive to get out of New York so why don't we take this opportunity and move on. Why don't you give Virginia a chance? I think you would like it there. It's a beautiful state, the people are very friendly and it's a lot safer than New York. I thought, wow, this is our chance to start over, start fresh and do it right. In the meantime, I continued seeking employment, but each day coming up empty-handed. It didn't take long for me to become busted, disgusted, totally broke and there was no one that I could rely on for assistance. It seemed as if the entire family was struggling for survival. I felt that God had placed me in a position where I had no other choice but to lean on faith. I stood at the window and admired the beautiful new car that I had just purchased while calculating my unemployment funds and realizing that there was no way I could make it like this. That night as I slept I envisioned that I was traveling on a bus to a place named Ports Mouth. The area looked familiar to me and for some reason in my spirit I knew that this place was home. The next morning I told my daughter of this vision and she began to laugh hysterically as she corrected my pronunciation. Mom, she said the name of the place is Port Smith and it's a little city in Virginia. I had no idea what God's plans were, all I knew was that I was about to lose everything, my home, my car and whatever little money I had left. I felt then that God was leading me to Virginia and I didn't put up much of a fight. My entire world was falling apart and I knew that I had to do something.

Several weeks later LaChelle and I took a trip to the place that we would soon call home. Having no idea what to expect or in which direction our future was going we set out to find some type of settlement in our lives. Marcus, who at the time didn't know that I knew that he was my son-in-law, was renting a small one-bedroom apartment, which looked like a garage that someone had converted into a storage unit. The windows were very drafty and the floor was weak and squeaky. LaChelle was preparing meals using an electrical hot plate and a microwave because there was no stove. The bathroom was only big enough for one person at a time parted by a folding partition used to form a door.

We dedicated the next few days to job-hunting. We dropped off applications at hospitals, employment agencies or anywhere we found advertised in the newspaper. We spent hours at the Virginia Employment Commission surfing the Internet and mailing resumes. We drove around and around from one apartment complex to another viewing living quarters, placing applications and inquiring. It seemed that by law no one would rent to us unless we could prove at-least six months of steady employment or supply six months of rental payments. After several days I sensed that Marcus was becoming uneasy with my presence so I decided it was time to make my way back to New York. We finally found one apartment complex that agreed to offer us housing with the presence of a co-signer. LaChelle explained to me that the apartment where Marcus resided was on a month-to-month rental therefore he wasn't tied to a lease and she would ask him to co-sign for us; Marcus agreed but made it apparent that he wanted to remain in his present status therefore he was not going to live with us. The thought passed my mind wondering how this situation was going to work, but since he was not aware of my knowledge of their marriage I just went along with the strategy with the hopes that things would eventually work its way out. I figured, when he felt comfortable enough; he would reveal the secret to me himself.

Upon returning to New York and in between hours of packing, I began applying on the computer for whatever position was available in the Tidewater area. LaChelle was especially excited about the move because, not only were we finally going to break out of the hustle and bustle of the fast-paced New York lifestyle, but she was a little closer to fulfilling her vision in discovering what married life was all about and that her son would finally become personally acquainted with his dad. She was proud of her husband and constantly spoke about her adoration for him. Marcus, however, still forbade her to tell anyone of the secret marriage. He made promises to her that they would wait until the "big June wedding" all-inclusive of a reception. The secret of this marriage was stabbing at my motherly instincts and the fact that he was determined to keep it that way was aggravating my consciousness and made me very uneasy. LaChelle has confided many things with me over the years confident that I would conceal every secret and I had never betrayed her before, but I was tempted to take a chance at that trust now. I wanted so badly to know why this was such a big secret. I kept looking at the engagement ring on her left hand and realizing that she was merely living out her fantasy. How could you possibly start a marriage with a lie and expect to be happily ever after?

My memory kept bringing me back to the whispering phone call in which she apologized for not allowing me be a part of this event and later how she explained that Marcus began the conversation that led to the discussion and a few days later she stood before the Justice of the Peace. I found the whole situation to be awkward because as far as I could see, Marcus was still struggling to love her and Marcus Junior. It might be understandable how a man could deny his child during pregnancy, but it boggles my mind how he could deny his son for the first two years of life then suddenly become the perfect father-husband figure overnight. Neither could I understand how a husband could send his wife home on an Am Trak for an eight-hour ride with no money in her pocket, to reach New York around one or two o'clock in the morning through a drug ridden, prostitution, high crime subway station carrying a baby and a stroller, dragging a suitcase all alone and yet vow to love her for life. Her excuse was always the same, "he said he doesn't have any money". Yes, I wondered what the marriage thing was all about, but I also realized that what was done was done. My daughter had now placed all her passion into this man and she trusted him to the full extent of her life. From then on she confided in him with every move she made to assure him that she was dedicated to him and him alone. It sometimes angered me because I felt that she told him much too much. Mom, she would say, "give him a chance", "I know that you don't trust him, but you just have to get to know him. You'll see he's not what you've made him out to be. He's really a nice person and you will find that out once you get to know him. Please ma, just give him a chance". I became so sick and tired of hearing that line, but I knew that Chelle was going to continue pursuing this relationship and the decisions that she was making. I felt that she was falling heart first too fast, but there was nothing that I could say or do at this point.

Today these words ring in my ears like the blunt-end of knitting needles; Jesus! What have I done? Why didn't I insist that she get away from him? Why did I even tolerate this garbage? I should have followed my instincts and bust his bubble right then, but I was afraid that if I had, I would have forever lost the confidence that my daughter had in me.

Anyway, let's get back to our plans to relocate to Virginia. Several days after our arrival back in New York my daughter received a phone call from her husband. His original plans to remain in the apartment that he now rented had come to an end when the fire department deemed that the apartment was illegal and could not be used for living quarters. I was then informed that Marcus would be moving in with us. I was not very comfortable with this idea, but since I could not get an apartment in Virginia otherwise, I wasn't left with much of a choice.

Besides, although he wasn't aware that I was aware, the fact still remains that he and LaChelle were legally married.

Taking everything I owned along with the little dignity I had left, I departed from New York on February 28, 2002. With my daughter and grandson in the car, we headed down Interstate 95. The furniture truck had already departed before us, driven by a friend. Along the way, whenever my daughter would find a pay phone, she would call to inform her husband of our location. When we arrived in Norfolk it took several phone calls to contact him. When she finally did, he explained that he was playing pool with some friends and perhaps didn't hear his cell phone ring. We stayed in a local hotel that evening and the next morning headed for the rental office to sign the lease and retrieve the keys.

The first few weeks in Norfolk were pleasurable. LaChelle had an expansive knowledge of the area and took delight in showing me around. The boxes were being unpacked and the house was beginning to look like a home. To my amazement the daughter that I had known to be untidy, nonchalance and free-spirited suddenly became the perfect wife, very neat and concerned about all family matters and activities. While I was used to automatically going into the kitchen and preparing meals for the family, I suddenly found myself not involved in the kitchen area at all while LaChelle made it a point to let me know that she wanted to cook for her husband. She did everything in her power to prove to him that she was worthy enough to be a wife and mother simultaneously. Although I was astounded to realize that marriage could change a person so suddenly, I was proud of her efforts. I constantly analyzed their attitudes towards each other out of curiosity of this fabrication and realized that LaChelle didn't seem satisfied, but determined to work it out while Marcus's behavior mystified my intelligence altogether. He acted as if her kindness towards him was what a wife should do in the act of submission, he walked around like he was the king of the castle acknowledging her presence when it was convenient and only acknowledging the presence of his son when she involved him in their plans. In my opinion, he acted as if the whole world revolved around and because of him. It wasn't easy, but I was strong-minded in staying silent hoping that LaChelle would figure out these things for herself.

It didn't take long to find employment. Several weeks later LaChelle was called by the Naval Exchange to begin employment with them. She was excited as she shared this information with her husband. Verbally he pretended to be happy about it but I saw displeasure upon his face. This is the first sign that detected to me a souring in the relationship and I knew that this was the point when LaChelle would see through his malarkey. He began to express his happiness for her while laying down his expectations. He expressed how proud he was of her and how satisfied he would be just to see her achieve some of the things that she enjoyed in life, but remember, he said, you as a mother have certain responsibilities that you have to take care of even if you work. First of all, he continued you know that the care of the baby is your responsibility; therefore you have to foot the expense of daycare or babysitting services out of your check. You also know that you need a car for transportation, which means that you will have to expense a car note, gas, insurance and maintenance. You also realize that it is your job to cook, clean, do laundry and keep the house up. I'm not trying to tell you these things to detour you, but I just want to make you aware where you stand. After you've covered your expenses, by all means, you can keep the remainder of your paycheck for yourself. I'm not expecting you to pay any of the bills in the house; I'll take care of those. Believe me, I'm happy that you want to work and I'm glad that you found a job. I'll pick you up until you get your car or you can take the bus. I'll even put the down payment on the car because I know that you are going to pay me back later. You said this job pays how much? Six fifty an hour? That's good; if you can cover all your expenses, by all means, go for it! Then he congratulated her with a kiss on the cheek. The expression upon her face let me know that she knew that he was messing with her head. She knew that there was no way that she could possibly uphold those responsibilities on that salary therefore she declined the position. Although I tried to enlighten her by reminding her that she and I were a team before and will always be a team, she couldn't understand why her husband who was suppose to love her would take her on such a mental guilty trip. Knowing that the going rate for jobs in the area is extremely low, I watched as my daughter became very puzzled upon how she was going to meet this obligation even if she were offer a job paying as much as ten dollars and hour. She knew and he knew that this was virtually impossible; therefore she began seeking other options to prevent this situation from reoccurring.

We found a little preschool/learning center, which was located on a dead-end street several blocks from our house. The owner of the learning center was very accommodating with our situation. My daughter and I explained to her that we were new to the community and did not have employment yet; therefore she arranged a very reasonable price that we could afford until our situation improved. LaChelle began calculating including the little money that she had been receiving in the past for child support and I agreed to cover the additional expense of childcare. When she mentioned this to Marcus with a smile he clarified that the child support money was reverted back to his paycheck now that the family was with him, and because this money was now a part of his check it was not an option for her. Although LaChelle continued to seek employment, she became very depressed each time she found that the salaries offered does not balance with the price of the economy in this area, therefore there was no way it would not meet the obligations that she was expected to uphold.

I began employment with the local healthcare center on April 15th. My duty assignment took me to Virginia Beach, which is approximately 30–45 minutes traveling time depending upon the traffic. I would get up in the morning, dress the baby, and drop him off at the learning center and head for work. When I arrived home in the evenings, my daughter often had dinner prepared on the stove. On the evenings that Marcus had duty she would ask me to go with her to the pass office to retrieve a pass in order to gain access to the base so that she could bring him something to eat. She explained that he often complained that the food, which was prepared aboard the ship, was not tasty therefore she was happy to be able to bring him food from home. This adventure ended about a month later when we went to the ship one evening to bring him food and found that he was not there because he did not have duty. She spent the remainder of the evening pacing the floor trying to figure out how she would approach him upon his whereabouts. This is the point when the real violence began.

You don't have a right to question me I heard him yell. What I do is my business and you stay out of it! Not only did that evening end with a physical fight, but with the confrontation of his alleged girlfriend who had no idea that he was married. As the days passed I was reluctant and afraid to go to work each morning because the arguments between the two of them had become so physically vicious and violent that I was afraid that someone was bound to come up dead. The telephone company was still dragging their feet about the installation of the house phone; therefore I had to purchase a cell phone, which I would leave home so that she would have access to make a call if she needed to do so. During my breaks or lunch hour I would call just to say hello or to give her someone to talk to. She spent many hours on the computer writing short stories and plays. She was in the midst of a book that she had dreams of one day publishing. From the time that she was a small child she would write short stories about incidents in school, on the playground or just amongst her friends and whenever she needed to pre-occupy her mind, she would go into one of her writing frenzies. I understood this attitude because writing was one of my escape goats also.

This particular day when I called, she answered the phone so abruptly and rude that I instantly became concerned and demanded and explanation. What do you want? She yelled into the receiver. Hello, I replied. "What's wrong?" I heard relief in her voice as she began explaining that Marcus had been calling her every few seconds and threatening her as to what he was going to do to her when he got home. That was the moment when I became very afraid for my daughter. I knew I had to work to keep up the rent, but I didn't know what I could do to help her. At the on-set of another confrontation between the two of them I decided to face Marcus to find out what the problem was. There was so much yelling between the two of them that I hardly understood anything that either of them was saying all I comprehended was that there was another female involved again. After a while, Marcus went downstairs and sat on the sofa. LaChelle remained upstairs for a while and I went back to my room. I was afraid to go to sleep because the two of them was still rustling around the house. I did not know if another fight was going to break out or what was possibly going to happen next. Because of the heavy violence I suddenly realized that this problem was not going to be fixed in the morning. My daughter entered my bedroom, retrieved my cell phone and walked out. She went down the stairs and out the door. I watched from the window as she disappeared into the darkness down the street. It was practically midnight and she was wearing a thin nightgown, no shoes, no robe and no underwear. I couldn't help but wonder where she was going like that or what her intentions were that she could become so angry to walk around outside at night in that manner. She was only gone for a short period of time, perhaps enough time to walk to the corner and back.

Marcus was lying, sleeping on the sofa when a white Pontiac Sunfire pulled up to the house. Two females got out of the car and approached LaChelle in a friendly manner. I had never seen these females before and had no idea what could possibly be going on now. LaChelle then led the two females into the house and towards the living room where Marcus was sleeping. I ran down the stairs not knowing what their intentions were and yelled at them from the stairs to stop before entering the living room. The sound of my voice woke Marcus and he looked up at the three of them and said to in a surprised groggy voice, what's going on? Who is this he said pointing to one of the females, and who is that he said pointing to the other. One female stepped closer as she replied, oh, you don't know me? No, he replied, who the heck are you? Why are you lying she replied. I've never seen you before in my life Marcus insisted as he became hostile towards the female that was boldly questioning him. As Marcus struggled to get on his feet the female began explaining the relationship between her and Marcus. She explained about the sexual encounters as she went on to describe the apartment at the other location, which is the one that we stayed at during our visits to Virginia before our relocation. She began to describe the entire apartment from the pictures on the wall to the location of each room and what furniture was located in each room. She even described what dishes were in the kitchen cabinet. It was obvious that she and other female had visited this apartment upon several occasions. It seemed that Marcus and his friends had been using this location for their wild, sexual affairs on the evenings that their wives expected them to have duty. She told my daughter of the evenings that involved alcohol as she described how they parted the mattress from the bed to make a place on the living room floor for one of his friends as well as which liquor bottles that were left in the apartment and the location of their remains.

LaChelle became extremely angry with her Marcus again, because earlier that day they had went to the location to retrieve some more of his belongings and while they were there she noticed liquor bottles around the floor and when she questioned him about these bottles he pretended to know nothing, yet, this female described every bottle that remained in the apartment after their encounter. After a few minutes DeMarco, one of Marcus's friend showed up, not knowing that he was walking into a trap because he was involved in the forementioned encounter with the other female that was present. It seemed that LaChelle had also called him. To his surprise the female called DeMarco by name and described everything that he was wearing on the night of their wild encounter even down to the color of his underwear. He, too, denied the whole situation. Marcus sided with his friend in agreement that these females were crazy. They tried convincing LaChelle that these were whores and admitted to picking them up in the mall. At this point I heard my LaChelle say to Marcus, so, you admit to knowing her? Marcus shook his head from side to side, threw his hands up in the air, sucked his teeth and walked away from them. The female stepped closer to Marcus as if she was provoking a fight. She screamed at him telling him that she was upset that he would disrespect her in that manner. She continued to explain that their sexual encounters which involved oral sex and unprotected intercourse.

For the next several days, weeks etc…this female and my daughter developed a strange sort of relationship, which made me very uneasy. This female explained to LaChelle that she knew of her existence, but she did know that the two of them were married. She explained how Marcus told her that Chelle was nothing more than his baby mama and that he had to support her and the baby because my daughter was a lazy, worthless nobody who did not have enough education to go out and get a job. She continued to explain how Marcus was talking marriage to her. Meanwhile, LaChelle also discovered another thrill that entertained Marcus involving a female in the New York area. She found that her husband was sometimes in the New York area when she was unaware of his arrivals. There were times when he would come to New York to visit the other female whom he had known for several years because she was the god-daughter of his father and there were times when he didn't even come to visit his son. This surely clarified the mysterious, unannounced, late night, extremely short visits that Marcus made upon his trips to New York. Those pop-up visits that was just enough to annoy the heck out of me. Those visits that he claimed consisted of errands and demands made by his father. He insisted that his dad ran a tight shift on the family and his times in New York were strictly consisting of family activities, but now I understand why his family activities never involved his son. I always thought that he had a way of treating my daughter as if she wasn't good enough for him. If she bought him a present, she would have to tell him what she was buying and how much she was paying for it before he decided whether or not he wanted to accept it. Even then, sometimes he would open a present and purposely leave it at the house as if he didn't want it. This is why, when she called me months later to tell me that they went to the justice of the peace and gotten married, I was baffled still and I wasn't understanding his sudden change of heart, or why she was forbidden to tell anyone of the marriage. Even though I never asked him about the ring that she was wearing I was curious as hell.

LaChelle began keeping the baby home during the day just so that she wasn't home alone. She had become so afraid of her husband that through fear she was practically trembling at the mere sight of his presence. She never knew, and neither did I, how the evening was going to end, which so often ended with several visits from the local police. I became so angry at the entire situation because I was in a situation where I could not reach out to her. For the first time in my life I felt totally helpless and angry because I'd come down here with her, leaving her without that option of escape.

It was a slightly chilly evening and I had just went to bed when I heard yelling, rustling of feet, moving of furniture, things falling and things being thrown from one end of the room to the other. I looked up and screamed, Jesus, not again! I tried to ignore them hoping things to work itself out, knowing that they were married, and sometimes-married couples go through arguments. I kept convincing myself and praying that it would be all right in the morning. After about a half hour, I had no other choice but to intervene. I opened the door of the room to find them hitting, punching and slapping each other. The room was in turmoil, furniture had been pushed out of its original context, there was broken glass all over the floor, the closet door was hanging off the rail and there were papers all around the floor. My presence in the room made very little difference to the situation. The baby had become so afraid that whenever the violence erupted he would run and jump on his mother's lap with hopes of protecting her. He didn't think his dad would hit his mom while he was on her lap, but I often found myself pulling the baby from between the two of them. Marcus showed no concern for the safety of his son during these outbursts. I was constantly trying to become a mediator in these situations, but soon found that I was wasting my time because I wasn't physically strong enough to intercede and neither of them was listening to me anyway. I became most afraid to go to bed at night because it seemed that this was the time when the violence would flare up. I couldn't make heads or tails of this situation in any kind of way so I often allowed my mind to drift back to their first physical fight to try and comprehend some sort of understand.

Marcus Junior watched helplessly as his mother fought for her life again and again. Each night he and I would lie in the bed listening and waiting for the moment when all hell would break loose in the other room. He would often say "Mama could I please go help mommy". I knew he meant well and he thought he really could help but he was much too small to do anything, as a matter of fact; I was almost as helpless as he was. My previous experiences led me to realize that my only weapon was dialing nine one one. I knew that calling the police would only delay the violence for a moment, but I learned to appreciate these few moments. I began to recognize the drill, the police would come, observe the situation, sometimes they would take notes and sometimes not, they would threaten to arrest someone take Marcus outside then leave. Each time that they come back, they would do the same thing. Whenever I tried to get involved they would use their knowledge of the legal system to alert me that I'm not involved and that this situation was between husband and wife. My only purpose for calling the police was to calm the situation for a moment. I also realized that whenever I announced that I was calling the police or had called the police, Marcus would immediately stop whatever it was that he was doing, go downstairs and wait calmly outside until they arrived. He would express to them that he was unaware of the problem and why his wife was so upset but as soon as they left, he would begin the battle again. There were times when I would call the police as many as three times a day. On one occasion I explained to the police that we had recently moved to Virginia and my daughter had no where to go, but the fights between the two of them had become so severe that I was afraid one of them was going to end up dead. I then suggested that they ordered Marcus to leave the house and not come back. I explained to them that he had friends that he could stay with; he also could have taken a place on the ship or in the barracks. I explained to him that I was concerned for the safety of both of them and the two of them immediately need to be separated. The police, once again explained to me that this issue was between husband and wife and that I was not a part of the situation, therefore I had no grounds to make a suggestion upon the outcome of this situation. From the top of the stairs LaChelle yelled her request to have Marcus removed from the house and the police went on to explain that the only way that they would remove him from the house would be to arrest him. I will press charges LaChelle yelled and the police escorted Marcus outside the house, left him standing at his car and then got into their car and drove away. The next morning I went to the renting office to inquire about changing the locks to the doors. The rental office informed me that, for as long as Marcus was listed on the lease, he was legally permitted to be on the premises and even if I changed the locks, if Marcus asked for a key that they would provide one for him. LaChelle became so afraid of the very man that she vowed to love for the rest of her life that her most invulnerable position was at the edge of the sofa, she would never sit back. She would position herself at the tip just in case she needed to rise to her feet quickly. Every day that household became an uneasy settlement for everyone who lived within those walls. LaChelle spent hours on the telephone trying to find a way out of this situation. She called every friend and family member that she could think of.

Today LaChelle called his company again begging for help. The company commander assured her that he would speak with Marcus about the situation and it was obvious that he did because Marcus came home that evening extremely upset and Chelle was his target of satisfaction. I was on my way home from work when I spotted Marcus's car traveling down Granby Street. It was obvious that he was going home, but I knew that this was not his normal route from work. Right then I sensed that something was wrong at home. I began to toot my horn to get his attention. I wanted to catch up with him to find out the details of the situation before I entered the house. It had become normal for me to walk into the house and find it torn apart because of the fighting between the two of them and calls to the police had become a daily routine. I was hoping that today would be different. I was hoping that I could at least once come home to a little peace and quiet. Marcus pulled over to the side of the road and I pulled behind him. He got out of his car and walked back to mine. Get in and sit down, I gestured him to the passenger side. He walked around and leaned into the window. I realized that he was not going to get in and I wasn't going to make a stink about it, I just wanted to talk. What's going on now I began? Well, he began. She's throwing a fit because the cable got turned off today. She's screaming and hollering about how little Marcus's only form of entertainment is watching cartoons and now he can't watch cartoons. Ms. Williams, he continued, I am so sick and tired of this. I work hard everyday trying to make her happy and all she ever wants to do is fight, everyday something different, now she's telling me that she doesn't want me in the house and that I can't see little Marcus anymore. Although these were the words coming from his mouth, I knew and he knew that the source of her anger was not because the cable got cut off, but the fact that he was so irresponsible. This little episode just added to the cut off notices that we had been receiving for the gas and the fact that she had found out that he had been driving around for years with no car insurance. Her question to him was what are you doing with your money? He wasn't paying the rent because I was doing that. He wasn't giving her any money and the baby hasn't had anything new. Was he still supporting his habits of entertaining females outside of the marriage? Is this why he can't handle his responsibilities?

One evening just as I arrived home from work LaChelle approached me requesting to go to the police precinct on Tidewater Drive, which was the only one we knew of at the time, in an attempt to retrieve an order of protection against Marcus. The officer that answered our knock at the door informed us that the precinct is only opened Monday through Friday nine to five and an order of protection is not issued from that office. He informed us to go to the precinct located on Virginia Beach Boulevard between 9–5 to apply. Because I was new in my employment and had not accumulated enough time to acquire a day off, I could not accommodate LaChelle for this inquiry. Upon several occasions I asked Marcus to remove himself from the house. Marcus had friends, who offered him a place to stay, but LaChelle had no place to go and he was well aware of that. LaChelle moved most of her belongings downstairs to the living room, which became a makeshift bedroom. She made it a point to have everything she needed before Marcus arrived home from work although Marcus had to pass through the Living room in order to access the bedroom. LaChelle made it a point not to even make eye contact with him because every single movement possibly erupted a reason for a physical challenge. LaChelle explained to me how she planted weapons in areas of the house for protection. She revealed to me that she had purchased a bottle of mace, which she kept either in her pocket or bra for protection, she explained how Marcus would enter the house during the day and overpower her with a physical brawl. She told me the story of how Marcus tiptoed into the house one day, went into the baby's room and attempted to tip down the stairs with him. When she began to wrestle him for the baby he told her that his father was coming to get him and was going to take him to Florida. LaChelle began placing folding chairs against the doors so that it would fall, making a crashing sound alerting her of Marcus presence. She refused to unlock the downstairs windows, even though the house was smothering hot. I would come home in the evening and find her and the baby still in pajamas because she was afraid to be caught in the shower, behind the curtain or standing in soap. She would not kneel next to the tub to bathe her son because this was also a defenseless position. During the times when I would take the baby to the park for a while, she would raise the blinds as high as they would hold as she sat in the living room in front of the window to make it accessible for all the neighbors to view the actions of the inside of the apartment. She would not leave the spot on the sofa where she was sitting, even to go to the bathroom until I returned. Within the matter of two months I watched my daughter change a vibrant, energetic, be-bopping young woman to a frightened, frail, shadow of a person. Even her physical appearance had changed, her skin had lost its shine and her face had no expression at all. Sometimes I would just watch her, not recognizing this person at all. She did not inform me about the threatening phone calls that she was receiving from the female in New York, but I found out one day when I answered the cell phone. The female was so huffy that she did not take a moment to ask for LaChelle; neither did she ask whom she was speaking with. "Listen, bitch, she blurted out, Marcus already told me what a lazy, no-good worthless piece of shit you are. Why don't you just go away and leave us the hell alone before I have to come down there and kick your ass". I just hung up the phone. I didn't even reply, neither did I tell LaChelle about the phone call. It was obvious that LaChelle was dealing with much more problems, threats and insults than she wanted to make me aware of. Fights between LaChelle and Marcus sometimes did not escalate for several days. These were the days when the two of them would walk around silent towards one another. That did not make the atmosphere any more settling because no one ever knew when, why, how or if a physical brawl was brewing.

One day LaChelle and Marcus left the house together in an attempt to go purchase the car that Marcus had promised to buy her. He'd already made the decision that when he got out of the military he was going to live in Florida around his family and he promised not to leave her without a way to get around. They were not gone for more than an hour when they returned in a heated argument. Campbell pulled up right behind them. LaChelle often called upon one of Marcus's friends for protection when she sensed the on-set of a physical conflict with Marcus. Most of the time she called for Campbell, maybe because Campbell was the one that she could be assured would come to her rescue. LaChelle walked into the door and headed for the upstairs. When I asked what was wrong she replied, "I'm going upstairs to take a nap". By now I understood that taking a nap was her way of escaping for a while. Then she looked at Marcus and replied, I don't want to fight with you anymore, I don't care what you do from now on, just leave me alone and leave me out of your mess. While downstairs, Marcus paced the floor for a few seconds and then headed upstairs behind her. I caught him by the arm and told him to leave her alone. As he snatched away he stated that he just wanted to talk with her, that he wanted to know what's wrong and he wanted to know if she was okay. I insisted that I was going upstairs to check on her and asked him to stay downstairs. When I reached the bedroom, LaChelle was lying across the bed on her stomach with her face buried into the crease of her elbow. I asked her if she was okay and she replied yes, "I just want to be alone for a while". Respecting her request I headed back down the stairs where I met Marcus as he was coming up. In an attempt to block him I insisted that he leave her alone, but my presence didn't seem to make a moment of difference. It was obvious that he was, once again, on a mission. He pushed pass me explaining that the wanted to speak with his wife alone for a few minutes. I didn't know what had happened to put LaChelle in this frame of mind, but I could clearly imagine what was about to take place. By the time I reached the kitchen I heard the two of them arguing. Then the scuffling of feet, dragging of furniture and breaking of glass and I knew that they were fighting again. I suggested that Campbell to go upstairs and break them up because I knew from previous experiences that the strength of my body weight and LaChelle's together was not enough to dominate Marcus's intentions. It only took a few minutes to come to complete silence and Campbell came back downstairs, sat in the chair nearest the door with a strange kind of look on his face. His body language told me that something bad had happened and he was wishing that he'd never gotten involved. The nervous and suspicious look on his face led me to believe that I needed to go check on my child. I hesitated to question him because I didn't want him leave until I returned. I needed him there not only for protection, but also as a witness to whatever had happened upstairs. I passed Marcus on the stairs; he immediately began to explain that LaChelle had taken a bunch of pills mixed with alcohol and is now motionless on the bed. I began to run up the stairs, but as I looked back over my shoulder I noticed that Marcus was reaching for his cigarettes and lighter, nonchalant, as if nothing was of his concern. When I reached the bedroom LaChelle was lying across the bed on her back motionless. Her eyes were closed and she didn't seem to be breathing. I tried to shake her and call her name, but there was no response. Immediately I grabbed the phone and dialed 911. I did not have time to access the situation even though I knew that LaChelle did not drink or smoke, neither was there enough alcohol in the house to do any damage to anyone or anything. Although I questioned this situation in my mind my main focus was handling the situation that was at hand. I kept trying to wake her until the ambulance arrived, but she never gained consciousness. As the EMT carried her down the stairs and out the door, Marcus was standing in the front yard puffing on a cigarette as if he was innocent and uninvolved. Campbell stood helplessly emotionless next to his friend with his hands in his pocket as he watched the ambulance take LaChelle away. He looked as if he was in total shock to what was happening.

I waited in the Emergency room at DePaul Medical Center accompanied by Marcus and Marcus Junior as the medical staff attended to LaChelle in the other room. About an hour later I was motioned by the hospital police officer to follow him into another room where he questioned me about the situation. This officer asked me what I thought happened and I told him just the way I saw it play out. He asked me about the relationship between my daughter and her husband and I explained to him about the constant fighting. He asked me if she fought him back each time they had physical contact and I responded, yes. He stated that they did not find any amounts of alcohol or drugs in her system, but according to the results of their tests they did find Marcus's thumbprints imbedded so deeply into her throat that cut off her breath, which caused her to lose consciousness. He asked me if I wanted him arrested and I replied by telling him that I want whatever it takes to stop the fighting between the two of them. Then he sent me back out to the waiting area and motioned for Marcus to follow him. Marcus then returned to the waiting area and sat down again. After a while he walked over to the counter and asked the receptionist if he could go to the back and see his wife. The receptionist replied that she would go to the back and ask and when she returned she told him that his wife requested not to see him. Marcus then got annoyed and asked me to drive him back home. I didn't mind because the baby was getting tired and wanted to sleep anyway. When I returned to the hospital, I requested to see my daughter and the receptionist motioned me through some doors and led me to where she was lying. When I reached the area where she lay, she was moaning and crying. The nurses were still waiting for more tests to return. When the tests returned, I asked the doctor in charge what the results were. She said the only problem that my daughter has is that she is extremely depressed. They prescribed her some medication and suggested that she contact the military Fleet and Family center to speak with a counselor about her depression. LaChelle sat quietly the entire ride home. She went into my bedroom and climbed into the bed, which is where she remained for the rest of the evening. The next morning, when she heard Marcus leave for work, she went and got into her own bed. I was relieved that today was Saturday and Marcus had 24-hour duty. LaChelle did not get out of bed the entire day, not even to go to the bathroom. I was concerned with this and kept coming in and out checking on her, bringing her food which she did not eat and asking if she needed assistance. She wouldn't eat and she wouldn't talk, she just lay there all day long. After a quiet evening I thought about getting up the next morning and find a church to attend but I was too afraid to leave the house. LaChelle was still in bed. I stood at the side of her bed and looking down at her. The positioning of her body let me know that she was in pain. I wanted so badly to talk with her, but the trip to the hospital was extremely excruciating and relatively long. I knew that she was drained mentally and physically, and needed the extra hours of sleep. I wanted so badly to talk with her. I needed to know all the inside details about what was going on. I needed to capture the pieces of the puzzle to this relationship that she had been hiding for so long. I knew that there had to be more to this madness than meets the eye.

Finally Monday rolled around and another call to his company commander which lead to another brawl. LaChelle had been making calls everyday begging for help, but today was different. The company commander told her that her husband was a good soldier and that's all that mattered. He continued with telling her how she should be proud of him and the way that he was putting his life on the line to protect and serve his country. That caught LaChelle by surprise and she didn't hesitate in letting him know how she felt about his comments. What the hell does that have to do with what I'm telling you she screamed into the receiver, I'm telling you that when he's suppose to be at work, he's here beating the hell out of me. How in the heck can he be a good soldier when he's not even there? I'm telling you that I think he's trying to kill me and all you could tell me is that he's a good soldier. You think I give a damn how good of a soldier he is and whether or not he's protecting his country? I'm tired of this man beating on me all day and all night. What kind of commander are you anyway, she yelled as she slammed down the receiver.

It was at that point that she realized that she was all alone, no help from the police, no help from the company commander, friends had stopped talking to her because they no longer wanted to get involved, the family had began to show no interest in this story anymore, yet nobody seemed to understand that she was still fighting for her life. Is it too late for prayer? Is God sick of this too? I went upstairs to find LaChelle sitting at the edge of the bed holding the bible. Beside her was the book that she had created and presented to Marcus in a last effort to resolve their differences and to show her love for him, a peace offering, and the same book that held all the sexy, loving inner emotions that she still held for him. Pictures of all the happy times, letters expressing their most intimate moments together, their secret sexual moments, her dream of a happy family, her dream of brothers and sisters for little Marcus and a poem about the in-laws that never knew that they were in-laws. I heard her and Marcus talking about the situation as she was telling him how her body was in so much pain from the confrontation of the previous fight that she could not move, he then replied again how he was so angry with her that he didn't care if she died.

Marcus came downstairs in his new Sean John velour sweat suit, wearing his new Jordan sneakers carrying a basketball beneath his arm. He brushed pass LaChelle as he informed her that he and his friend DeMarco were going to shoot a few hoops and he would be back soon. LaChelle watched as he got into the car and drove away. Without saying a word she went upstairs to her room and closed the door. The volume of the television was extremely loud and I knew that she was thinking the same thing that I was thinking. Why would he put on a hundred dollar sweat suit, a hundred dollar pair of sneakers and then pick up a dirty basketball talking about going to shoot hoops; I wouldn't dare ask the question though. When Marcus returned, hours later, LaChelle questioned him about his actions and they began arguing again. Thank God, this argument didn't result in a physical fight. I learned to be grateful for the few moments of quite between brawls. I pretended to be going to the bathroom so that I could come upstairs and not look so obvious that I'd come to check on Chelle. Although she was sitting in front of the television the expression on her face let me know that she wasn't really watching it and her mind was a million miles away while the baby lay sleeping in her arms.

It was late in the evening when I came up the stairs and heard Marcus on the telephone. When I reached the top of the steps I peered through the crack in the bedroom door and observed him sprawled across the bed entertaining some female. When he spotted me, he jumped up and changed his tone of voice as if he was casually speaking to one of his male friends. He gave me a cunning smile as he walked towards the door, politely nodded and closed the door tightly. I was upset, but grateful that it was me who caught that scene and not LaChelle. A while later I heard his cell phone ring. He was walking around outside talking with his dad. I took advantage of these moments as if God was sending down small blessings a trickle at a time. This meant a few moments of peace and quiet and a few moments for my daughter to gather herself. LaChelle was desperately looking for a way out of this situation. She began a more diligent seek for employment. She just wanted to get out of the house during the day and she was hoping for a job that allowed her the hours that worked around my schedule so that I could take her to work in the mornings. Picking her up in the evenings didn't matter because either she would wait on me or I would wait on her to bring her back home. Because LaChelle had two previous car accidents within the past two years she had difficulty obtaining car insurance. The insurance company would not allow me to place her on my policy within a reasonable charge and because of regulations of the insurance company, LaChelle and I was not allowed to reside in the same household as far as the insurance company was concerned. I knew she felt like a sitting duck in the middle of hunting season trapped in the midst of the forest with no place to go, so when Marcus started to tell her that he would place her on his insurance as a second driver she accepted his offer until she could do better. It wasn't exactly what she wanted, but at this point, she had run out of options.

Things were beginning to look up for LaChelle. Today she received her income tax check and she had found employment with a temporary agency located somewhere on Military Highway and looking forward to begin working on Monday, June 24th. At that point it didn't matter what the pay consisted, she just needed to be out of the house so she could clear her head and find things to do to move on with her future. On Thursday, June 20th, LaChelle's friend took her to Virginia Beach to make a down payment on a vehicle that LaChelle had chosen to purchase.

I had just put the baby down to sleep, but by the position of is little body I knew that the he too was hurting inside. I knew that his spirit was broken and what hurt the most was the thought of knowing that there was nothing that either of us could do about it. He too knew that at any moment now, his mother was once again about to enter into a fight for her life. I knew that in his mind he could picture his dad's fist connect with his mother's body again and again. I just sat there, in the dark, at the edge of my bed confused, angry, helpless and alone wondering what's going to happen tonight. How will I be waken and at what time? Will this be another night that I spend dialing 911 over and over again? Will tomorrow be another day that I sit at my desk at work with my mind disconnected from my body due to exhaustion. Will I once again come running from my room in an unsuccessful attempt to peel Marcus's body off of my daughter's? Peace and quiet only lasts for a moment. I found myself drifting into prayer, Lord Jesus; you know what the situation is here. I really have no idea, but Lord please let me know what I can or should do. Suddenly my prayer was broken by a faint whisper. Mom, mom, come here. I heard my daughter's voice beaconing in the darkness. I took one deep breath, rose from my bed, and walked into my daughter's room. She was sitting at the foot of her bed starring into mid air. She looked as if her mind was a million miles away. The expression on her face let me know that she was in despair. What's the matter, I asked. Mom, I need you to pay attention. I was confused for a moment. Attention to what? She continued, you know Marcus is outside on the phone with his father, right? Yea, and, I replied. She paused for a moment. I was waiting for her to tell me something that I didn't know. I already knew that every time Marcus gets a call from his dad he goes outside for privacy. I never knew why, but I assumed that that was normal practice for that family. It didn't bother me none. As a matter of fact, those were the few moments of quiet that gave me a little relief in the interval of the arguing and fighting. She continued Mom haven't you realized by now that every time he speaks with his dad he comes back into the house in a rage? He's going to beat the hell out of me for absolutely no reason. Mom, I don't know what the issue will be this time, but I'm sure he will think of something before he gets back in here. And if he can't think of anything, I'm sure his dad will help him out.

It suddenly dawned on me. How stupid have I been? How could I not have realized this before? How could I have not realized that his dad was calling me for information in between all the "I feel so bad that you have to be there in the middle of all of that", the "I'm praying for you" and the "I'm trying to tell my son to stop"? Now that I think about it, she right. Oh my God! Most of their fights did begin right after those phone calls. How could I have been so naive to this whole set-up? Is his dad a part of this scene or is Marcus using his dad as a prop to build his anger. I knew that his dad didn't like my daughter due to previous encounters. The day that his dad called me to inquire about our existence in Virginia, I knew that there were lies that had been told. His dad wanted to know from me, what kind of mother would allow her daughter to drop out of college to follow a man in hopes of a relationship. It's obvious that his son had been telling him that my daughter was stalking him. Did it ever dawn on his father that they were married? Never, his son was so perfect that he believed anything that his son told him. I knew that he was the type of father that accused everyone around for his child's wrongdoings, but I just assumed that he had enough brains to put two and two together. Suddenly my mind went back into prayer. Lord Jesus, I need you NOW!

Go mom, go. My daughter was shoving me out the door; he's coming, you have to go. Come with me, I begged. You can sleep in the bed with the baby and me, there's enough room, and you don't have to be in here when he gets here I begged. No mom, I can't do that, that will not stop him. Just go, I'll be okay, I'll stand up to him, I'll let him know that I'm not afraid of him, I'll be okay, just go! A final shove left me standing at the top of the stairs when he reached the top. I looked him directly in his face. He gave me a fraudulent nod, a crooked smirk from the corner of his mouth and walked pass me towards his bedroom. With his left hand he pushed the door behind him in an attempt to close it, but the door bounced off the frame and rested in a position, which allowed me to view the actions of the bedroom. I watched as he positioned himself directly in front of her in a threatening manner. Then I heard that famous question, "Why did you tell my father that we were married and why did you tell my father…?" I knew that he was talking between his teeth because it blurred out the ending of the sentence. At that moment he raised his hand and with one blow he slapped her so hard that her body uprooted from the bed and bounced to the other side. Thank God that she had positioned herself that she wouldn't fall to the floor. She struggled to get her feet on the floor while swinging back at him. I ran into my room and grabbed the cell phone to dial 911. Then I heard another small voice say, Mama, can I please go help mommy? There's nothing that you could do sweetheart, I replied. You're much too small, but Mama is calling the police again. They will be here in a minute to help mommy. I'm calling 911 now, I screamed.

Within a few minutes Marcus was headed down the stairs. That was the response that I waited for. I knew that because Marcus was in the military the last thing he wanted was to get arrested. 911 had become the only strength I had against the situation because I knew that calling the police was basically a waste of time. Just like all the other calls for help, I expected the police to walk in with their supremacy mannerism looking harmonized with legal authority, standing wide-legged placing one hand on their hip and the other on their gun while holding a stern look on their faces as if they were going to conquer the situation. It looked like a scene from an old western movie when the Marshall walks in, draws his gun, shoots the bad guy, blows the smoke from the tip of his weapon, spins it and returns it to his hoister. But the only difference between this scene and that one was the fact that the only weapon of authority carried in this scene was an ink pen and small three-by-five writing pad. The only threat that these lawmen possessed was the threat of an arrest. It didn't take much thought to realize that the only reason the police showed up were to have something to do during working hours and the only reason they carried a pen and pad were to note their whereabouts for the purposes of timekeeping and payroll and their only legal knowledge was to let me know that I had no rights in this situation as a parent. The police realized that the less time that they spent inside the dwelling was the more that they could give the impression of being uncompromising, heroic and authoritative in the eyes of the rubber-necking neighbors that were only hoping to peek in on some action for the benefit of getting their faces on the local news. While my child was fighting for her life, the police acted as if they were inadvertently hoping for an opportunity in Hollywood. I had been through the scene so many times that by now I knew the routine. Upon the arrival of the police, Marcus would be either sitting on the stoop or standing against the car looking calm as if nothing happened. He would always motion the police towards his wife telling them that she's ranting and raving for reasons that he didn't understand and the police walked in looking important, pulled out a three-by-five pad, wrote down something, returned it to his top shirt pocket and walked out with their heads up and chest out as if they had everything under control.

It's been several years since Farrah Fawcett won an Oscar for her performance in the movie "The Burning Bed" and in as much as I was trying not to compare the two situations, I realize that the law has not made much progress to control these crimes. It almost seems as if they don't even care. Even in that movie, Farrah Fawcett experienced relief during the hours that her husband was at his place of employment; unfortunately LaChelle did not have that opportunity. Perhaps because he was a soldier and some how felt confident that he had access to the invisible circle of protection that's created by the world around him who viewed his efforts as heroic as if he's laying his life on the line to save his country 24/7. After the first month I saw how the wear and tear of mental, physical and spiritual stress began to decompose Chell's soul. It wasn't only the depth of the abuse, but the consistency of the batter. It was as if she was P.O.W. practice at the onset of the mentions of the war in Iraq. The nonstop abuse became total destruction of a love that was once so deeply cherished. A dream shattered like tiny fractures of a broken mirror that still reflects a future that will never be. It took only two short months in the hands of the man that so tenderly drew her into his web of deceit to seize the gift that God gave to me and rip it to shreds. She reached up, but nobody reached back. She soon found that she had nothing to grip and her life was slowly seeping away. She held her head up as she continued looking for a miracle, praying that somehow God would pull her through, and with this prayer in her heart she once again trusted the man that vowed to love for better or worst not knowing that today just might be the day that death would do them part.

The following Sunday was calm, it was Father's day and LaChelle had just returned from New York where she was grateful that her friend had graduated so that, while she had a chance to go attend the graduation, she also had a chance to scrutinize the family for a place to hide out for a few weeks. At the time, I had a pretty good idea what her reasons were for making the trip to New York knowing that it wasn't only for the purpose of the graduation. I also knew that she too just wanted a weekend of non-violence. Upon her return she began to tell me how one cousin's home was an open house where people just walked in and out all day and all night long. She explained to me how she was asleep on the sofa and woke up with one of his friends standing over her looking down at her as if she was fresh meat waiting to be cooked. She told me how another cousin had said to her "no bitch sleeps under the same roof with my husband but me". I knew my child was in serious trouble and all I could say was, oh my God. Father, please help!

It has been almost a week now without a single trace of an argument or a physical fight. It was now Saturday morning, June 22nd. I was wakened by the spirit of Uncle William. LaChelle did not know Uncle William because he passed away years before she was born, but I had told her many stories about him, so when I told her that his spirit had come to visit me she became very alert. He told me, I began, that I can lean on him. He told me that God had made a decision and one of us will be leaving this house. This was the second visit from Uncle William. Last Saturday I woke up to someone poking me in the side. Knowing that everyone close to me knew that I wasn't ticklish, I knew it had to be someone who had not been around me since childhood. I'd recognized him from the waist down, just as I'd done when I was a child. All he said then was "you can lean on me".

I'd planned to get up early to catch the bank when they opened at 9:00 but I got involved with straightening up the house and didn't get to the bank until an hour later. I walked into the bank to find the usual Saturday morning crowd that backed the line up from the teller's desk, twisted a few times and stopped a few feet short of the door. About an hour later I made my way to the Dollar General store where I walked around for a while, picked up a few household things before returning home. The last few days were extremely hot and it was obvious that this morning was not going to be any different. LaChelle had wakened up in an unusually happy mood. She had been so miserable and depressed for the last few months that I was pleased to see her in this frame of mind. She opened her closet and withdrew a blue denim skirt, the kind that hung right above her knees with the six-inch split up the front. She placed the skirt neatly on the bed and turned to her dresser where she pulled out a light blue spaghetti-strapped blouse. She began looking around the room scanning for shoes to match. Somehow I knew that she was going to choose her favorite slip-ons. She gathered her Victoria secret's shower gel with the matching lotion and sat them on the corner of the bathtub where she was preparing to shower. She went down the stairs into the kitchen and plugged in the iron and sat up the ironing board. Reaching for the starch, she pressed the skirt first, placed it carefully across the back of the chair then ironed the blouse. The shower water ran for a long time so I knew that she was taking her time making it a point to not only look good, but also to smell good. Once out of the shower she began hot-curling her hair. Marcus walked pass her again and again as he glanced in her direction with a disgusted look upon his face. Neither of them was speaking because of the bitter fights that they had become accustomed to for the past few weeks. LaChelle had explained to me just a few days ago how she was confused about the exact nature of the problem. The initial problem had passed, but the anger seemed to linger. At this point LaChelle had accepted the fact that this relationship was over and there were no chance of recovery.

This was the day that LaChelle had made plans to go pick up the car that she had previously chosen. She had already placed a down payment on it and all she needed was to show proof of insurance. She was exceedingly happy as she bopped around to the rap station on the radio. I noticed that Marcus just walked out and sat in the car as LaChelle and I teased around for a while, joking about her new wheels. I said, "Oh, now that you're gonna have your own wheels you're not gonna want to hang with me anymore huh?" "Yea right ma, the only thing that's going to change is that now we'll be riding to the mall in my wheels and not yours". When I get back that's what we'll do. Then she kissed the baby good-bye, blew me a kiss and headed towards the door. LaChelle, I interrupted, are you sure you don't want me to take you to get your car, I asked. No Ma she replied, Marcus is going to put me on his insurance as a second driver; therefore he has to take me. Do you have your pepper spray I asked? With a snicker she reached down between her breasts, flashed the tip of the bottle, pushed it back and walked out the door. I watched as she half walked, half skipped to the car. For some reason I took a second look at her outfit, probably because she looked so nice. Her baby blue tee strapped blouse that ran ruffles around her neck sat perfectly with the blue jean knee length skirt and slip on shoes. Her hair was parted in the middle and fell down the side of her face with curls at the tip that lay so perfectly right below her chin. She was absolutely gorgeous and the glow of her spirit made her that much more beautiful. I stood at the kitchen window and watched the car as they pulled out of the parking spot. That moment was interrupted with Marcus Junior saying "Mama, I'm hungry". "Do you want a grilled cheese?" I asked knowing that this was his favorite food. I reached for the bread and opened the refrigerator to retrieve the butter, pulled a pan from below the cabinet, turned the fire low and proceeded to make a grilled cheese sandwich. Marcus Junior positioned himself on the carpet in the middle of the living room floor right in front of the TV as courage the cowardly dog discovered ways to save his beloved owner from whatever danger was lurking. Do you want strawberry milk or chocolate milk I asked knowing that he was going to say strawberry. I took time to remove his shoes so that he could relax and when the grilled cheese and milk was prepared I placed in in-between his open legs. Marcus Junior had just taken his second bite of the sandwich when the phone rang. I got up and walked to the phone and picked it up. Hello. The voice coming through the receiver was in a panic. I immediately recognized the voice; it was Marcus.

"Ms. Williams", he said, "you have to come right now. Something happened. It looks bad, it looks real bad". What happened I said? He continued to say that she jumped from the car while he was driving. Where are you, I asked? We're by the gate. You know, gate four. My mind began to race. Gate four is less than a quarter of a mile away. I hung up the phone, grabbed Marcus Junior, put his shoes on and ran to the car. I went up by gate four and saw nothing. I began traveling down the street towards the highway entrance where I saw a crowd of people, an ambulance and a police car. When I reached the scene the paramedics was picking LaChelle up from the ground on a stretcher and placing her in the ambulance. The ground had a huge bloodstain. Marcus was talking to the police officer. The first thing I noticed was that he had the wedding ring on his pinky. This was an obvious sign to me that there had been a physical fight between the two of them. Every time that they had a physical fight, LaChelle would remove her wedding ring and throw it at Marcus. After the ambulance announced to me that they were taking her to Virginia Beach General I walked over to Marcus who was basically mumbling. I left him there talking to the police and I headed for the hospital. I don't know exactly how long they were gone from the house, but I know that it wasn't more than ten or fifteen minutes. Once again, I was put into a situation where I didn't have time to assess the situation, I had no other choice but to attend to the problem that was at hand at the moment.

While at the emergency room I pace the floor back and forth waiting for results or word about the condition of my daughter, praying for a miracle. At first the medical staff would not give me any updates. Each time that they came to look for family members they requested to speak with the husband and were told that he wasn't there. I am the mother, I requested, please tell me something; I'm sorry, they'd say, this is between husband and wife and we cannot release any information to you without the husband's permission. After about a two-hour wait, a clergyman motioned me into a side room. While in the room he revealed to me that LaChelle was not going to survive. He said that her injuries were too extensive and that I should begin making funeral plans immediately. He was very cold-hearted, unconcerned and to the point. I couldn't understand this type of attitude coming from a man of his stature. When I requested to speak with a doctor he insisted that the doctors were much too busy to speak with me, he continued with telling me that they didn't expect her to live for more than eight to twelve hours. At that moment another man entered the room. He wasn't a doctor either, but another clergyman. He introduced himself to me and explained that he was associated with the military. He was more comfort to me than anyone I had encountered that entire day. I walked out of that room with my grandson by the hand in total shock. It was hard to bring myself to believe that this was happening when just a few hours ago my daughter and I had just made plans to spend the day at the mall.

All types of thoughts began racing through my head as I tried to figure out why. How could a person who wasn't suicidal, never before been suicidal suddenly decide to commit suicide for no apparent reason? I tried to make sense of it all, but kept coming up blank. Using my cell phone, I then began calling the family. Everybody was in total astonishment. I'm sure they were trying to figure this out in their minds as well. The entire scene made no common sense at all. I found myself standing in the middle of the yard area outside of the emergency room with my hands up saying, "Lord, Why?" Once again, I am left with the task of just handling the situation that is at hand. Being new to the area, I had no idea how to go about planning a funeral. I need a funeral home, a burial ground, a minister to perform the services, I have to buy a coffin, what is she going to wear, how do I go by informing everybody of what just happened and most of all, how do I tell people that my mentally healthy child just committed suicide for no apparent reason. While I was trying to figure all of this out in my head I happened to look up and across the parking lot I saw her husband making his way towards us.

Another hour had passed when I was informed that LaChelle had been taken and placed in a hospital room. I was lead up to that room where she had been placed, hooked up to several machines, some beeping and some humming, the respirator, breathing for her because she no longer had the ability to breathe on her own, her eyes were slightly opened and held an unresponsive stare. I watched, as she lay there motionless. Her body seemed to reveal a strange kind of peace as if she didn't have a care in the world. Her body was very cold to the touch and although there was a heated blanked atop her, her hands and feet were ice cold. Somehow I knew then that she was gone, there was no warm blood running through her body. At first I thought not to let her son see her in that state, but he requested that he wanted to see his mother, therefore, I brought him in. He touched her face, he touched her lips he requested me to lift him higher because he wanted to touch her hair and then he said, "Mama, mommy needs a teddy bear". I couldn't help but wonder, what he was thinking at that moment. I knew that LaChelle couldn't talk, but could she hear us? I know that at that moment she was very saddened at the idea that she couldn't communicate with her son. What do you say to a three year old who wishes to stroke his mother's hair as he watches her die? For a young child, he had a very broad understanding of the entire situation. The only thing left to do now is wait. Wait for that moment when the doctor would finally pronounce her dead.

I took this time out to leave the hospital for a while to take Marcus Junior home in hopes that he would lie down and take a nap. He was very saddened by the entire scene, realizing that his mother was gone forever. He fell asleep in the car and I carried him into the house. He was very restless. He tossed and turned a lot and he didn't sleep for long. The moment he awoke he asked to go back to the hospital to see his mommy. I don't know if it was a blessing that he understood so well, or if it would severely affect him in the future. I began an extensive cleaning process knowing that in just a few hours my house would be filled with people. Family and friends both would be coming in from other states. They would need hotel information or directions to the nearest hotel. How do I direct them? I really have no idea what just happened so what do I tell them? There is no way I could explain this. How do I live without my only daughter? What do I do without my best friend? I am suddenly alone. Alone in a state that I know nothing about. No family, no friends. I barely know my way around the neighborhood. What's going to happen now? Do I stay in Virginia? I knew that going back to New York was not an option for me but where do I go? Where do I start with making funeral plans? I then pulled out the yellow pages and began running my finger down the funeral home column. What type of life insurance is there? Does he have life insurance on his wife? If not, how do I bury her? I just exhausted every dime I had to relocate to this state, get and apartment, begin new auto insurance etc. What's going to happen to my grandchild now? What if family can't come up with enough money to help me out? What do I do? One option is that the money that she had in her purse to purchase her car was still there. Looks like I might have to bury her with her own money.

It must have been God that took control of the wheel because I don't remember doing much driving, but I found myself pulling into the parking lot of the hospital. The hospital suddenly looked very dark and dreary. I was pulling into the parking garage with Marcus Junior in the back seat when I noticed familiar faces gathered at the front entrance of the hospital. I was not close enough to hear the conversations, but was close enough to view the motions. Marcus was leaning casually against a pole puffing on a cigarette, surrounded by several male figures as if it were a gathering outside a local club. Marcus did not seem to be grieved at all while he was socializing, laughing and slapping five with friends while just a few floors up his wife was still fighting for the last moments of her life. I was curious to hear what they were saying, but I knew if I got closer he would catch a glimpse of me and the crying scene would instantly develop again and just as I'd predicted when he noticed that Marcus Junior and I were walking towards him, just like the switching of a light, the tears began to flow. While trying to ignore the drama, I walked passed s if I hadn't noticed a thing. The minister that was associated with the military was waiting at the door for my arrival. I began wondering what I would have done without him. This man must have been heaven sent because he did not leave my side. Once again, standing by my daughter's side, there was no change in her condition. I kept asking the nurses what were their opinion of the assessment of the situation hoping for a miracle and they kept telling me that chances were very slim to none that she would not live and even if she did, she would be in a vegetable state and the stare in her eyes would be there for the rest of her life. Looking down upon my daughter lying there so peaceful, motionless and blank, I prayed at that moment that God would go on and take her. Her son was still playing in her hair and kissing her on the cheek. The tube that was taped to her lips held her mouth in an open position. The machine on the wall was beeping as the lifeline rose and fell. Her chest expanding and deflating as the pressure pump goes up and down. I knew then that this was the end. I knew that my baby was gone. Marcus sat in a chair on the other side of the bed and watched as every drop of life slowly seeped from her body. I was angry with him, I was angry with myself, I was angry with God and I was angry at the entire world, but what could I do? Anger was not going to resolve the situation. At the back of my mind I kept thinking, when this is all done and over, the police will handle it. They know about the previous attempted murders against her. They know about all the fighting. His commander can witness to the problems, desperate phone calls and physical contact between the husband and wife upon several occasions. There was too much evidence for him to get away with this. The waiting went on for hours. My cell phone rang every five minutes or so, somebody wanting to know what's going on now. I knew that the entire family was praying for a miracle and so was I. I prayed that LaChelle would at least live long enough to tell me what happened.

It had already begun to get dark outside and Philip was pulling into the parking lot of the hospital. I knew the trip from North Carolina was not easy for him under these circumstances. I saw on his face that he was destroyed. His closest playmate was gone. The only sister he grew up with was gone. His best friend was gone. There was nothing that I could tell him at that moment. What was done was done. I knew that he felt the same anger as I did. There was nothing more that we could do for her now. I was standing in the midst of a situation that I had no explanation for. The only one that I could think to blame was myself. I should not have let her go with Marcus that morning. Somehow I felt the vibes in his actions that gave me a chill deep within my soul. But never did I think he would be capable of such a cruel act of hatred. After all, this was her high school sweetheart, the escort to her sweet-sixteen party, the father of her child and most of all, her husband, her lover, and her best friend.

As a single parent I knew that it was my job to protect my children as much as life would allow. There were some tough times, but nothing that we didn't work our way out of. Never have I ever had to witness her fight so hard at anything. Since her marriage, she fought her hardest just to stay alive and there was nothing that I could do to help her. Suddenly I felt as if I was trapped in a box and all sides had fell down on me the pressure was so enormous leaving me with no way out. Never was I more confused. I found that I was not as strong as I thought I was mentally, physically, emotionally, spiritually or financially. I also found that family and friends were not strong enough, loving enough or believing enough to simply open up their hearts, minds or homes. I felt all alone and the question kept running through my head, why? Why, Lord, Why? Many nights I sat awake in the dark wondering if God had departed along with everyone else. Had God become so outraged at me that he turned his back and chose to ignore my cries? Why was he allowing Satan to trample my world? What did I do that was so wrong? I'm not a murderer, I'm not a thief, and I'm not a home wrecker neither am I a drug addict. What would cause God to take such drastic measures?

It was about 2:00 in the morning when the doctor and the two ministers entered into the waiting area and motioned for Marcus to come with them. When I stood to my feet I was informed by the hospital minister that they only wanted to speak with the husband and I was to stay put until they call for me. I insisted on coming, therefore Marcus agreed. At this moment, I was tired of being treated as if I were invisible. I didn't want to hear any more explanations about how, in the state of Virginia, the husband has jurisdiction and the parents has no rights. I don't want to hear anything else about how no decision will be made except by the husband. At this point, I'm angry enough to tear the world apart with my bear hands if I possible could. I was totally and completely sick of the rudeness of the hospital minister and by the looks on my face I'm sure he got the message.

The announcement was not made until we reached the room where my daughter was. Besides the two ministers and some medical staff there were people whom I did not recognize. "Mr. Harris, your wife has passed away". They then went on to explain that the last brain wave test showed no sign of activity, therefore, they will be releasing her from the respirator. At that point I felt that my life was over. I felt that I didn't have anything more to live for. Had it not been for the fact that I still have Philip and Marcus Junior, my chances for survival were very slim. One of the men in the room began rambling something about donating organs. He began asking questions like, what requests did she have for organ donation? What's written on her driver's license about donating organs? Nobody seemed to care that I just lost my child. Everybody had a job to do and they wanted to do it at that moment. I heard someone ask do you want an autopsy just as the hospital minister reminded me that all decisions were to be made by the husband, my only thought was to smack the hell out of him. Thank God for the military minister who stepped in between us and put his arms around me and led me back down the hallway towards the waiting room where Philip, his pregnant girlfriend and Marcus Junior was waiting. From the look on my face when I entered the room, Philip knew that his sister was gone. I couldn't even get the words out. My family was forever destroyed. How could a day that started out so sunny and bright actually turn out to be the darkest Sunday ever?

I tried to sleep that night, but the atmosphere in my home was restless. I gave Philip the bedroom and I pulled the two sofas together to make a bed for Marcus Junior and myself. I had no idea where Marcus was, not that I cared, but I knew that he had enough friends in the area to find a place to go. But he was smart, he chose to find a way to have himself admitted into the psychiatric ward at the Norfolk Naval Shipyard hospital. One of Marcus Junior's favorite things to play with was the scrunchy that I wore in my hair that held my ponytail together. He liked to put it around his forehead and play karate man. When he pulled the scrunchy from my hair I knew that this is what he was going to do with it. At this moment, I would let him have the entire world if it would comfort him for just a second. We then dozed off to sleep. I was awakened by what felt like a hit on the arm of the sofa that was closest to my head. It felt as if someone had hit the sofa with their hand. I jumped up and noticed that Marcus Junior seemed to be having problems breathing. His breathing was very deep and very heavy. Then I noticed that the scrunchy was around his neck. For some strange reason I was comforted in knowing that my daughter's spirit was watching over us as we slept.

It puzzled me as to how, by Virginian Law, all my rights as a mother were taken away. Over and over again the police kept reminding me how I was not a part of the violence as if I didn't even live in the house. This situation is between husband and wife is what they kept repeating over and over again. It's funny how I now have rights. I have the right to bury my child. The company commander did not care enough to take control of his soldier. The police did not care enough to arrest the man that the hospital discovered and admitted to attempted murder against his wife.

After just a couple hours of sleep, I began the day with trying to bring all those questions in my mind to a reality, first things first. What do I do now? Who do I call? Where do I go? How do I start? I guess I need to begin with writing an obituary. So I turned on the computer and began to type. I pulled out LaChelle's important paper case and began tracking the years of her life. All that I didn't know, I knew that somebody would fill in, information such as the names of aunts, uncles, cousins and other family members on her father's side. After completing the obituary and putting it aside I began typing the funeral program. Who will sing? Who will preach? Who will pray? It wasn't long before the phone rang. It was the military minister. He gave the name and address of a funeral home in Hampton. Thank God for that minister. I don't think I would have made it without him. I pray that God forever smiles upon him.

THE POLICE REPORT

Funeral plans were in the process. Mr. Harris, his wife and two youngest children who were lodged in a hotel in downtown Norfolk accompanied me to the funeral home. Mr. Harris has been standing close by his son's side since his release from the Psychiatric ward. The scenes from the previous day were replaying themselves over and over again in my head as the funeral director led us through all the details of the final arrangements.

The funeral and burial was both set for Wednesday. Marcus acted as if he was much too grieved to offer any sort of support. All of the parental rights that I had been stripped of suddenly became available to me. I had every right to make the funeral and financial arrangements as Marcus repeated over and over again how there was no life insurance policy and he had no money to offer to this cause; It' funny how I never once heard anyone tell me that this was between husband and wife only. I spent the next few days shopping for a burial outfit, checking make-up and making sure that my baby was just as beautiful dead as she was when she was alive.

I can't for the life of me understand how so many people got word of the funeral so soon. The Funeral services were comforting; the church was filled with all of LaChelle's friends from New York. The church that I had been a member since childhood and that my LaChelle had served faithfully as a youth usher drove a van down from New York with members that lovingly involved themselves in the services. The police processional from the church to the burial grounds made my daughter appear as if she was a celebrity of some kind. The Lord giveth and the Lord taketh away was the words spoken as the final rose pedals lay atop the coffin as everyone began to disperse. Marcus and his family observed the services from the farther end of the gravesite. I kept convincing myself that there was no way he was going to walk away from this; there was much too much evidence for the police to not arrest him. I guess I was hoping that when the services were over the police would surely show justice for LaChelle. I prepared myself for the long court appearances and testimonials to the ordeals as I had witnessed time and time again. Marcus and his family got into their car and drove away.

It's been four days now since the burial. I decided to go back to work because I figured it would take my mind off of the present situation and at least for eight hours a day I would be forced to think about other things. I was curious to find how the police report was worded, hoping that I could find some answers. I decided to use my lunch hour to take a trip down to the precinct and pick up the police report. I wanted to know why the police did not arrest Marcus for this fatal crime, but instead permitted him the freedom to travel to another state. The police overlooked the previous attempted murder, which was recorded by the emergency staff at DePaul Medical Center. They also overlooked the previous domestic violence calls to 911. Perhaps they are waiting for him to return from Florida for further investigation. But meanwhile, I needed answers now.

The lobby of the precinct was very dimly lit. There were people sitting on benches that had been lined against the wall at the right side of the room. One woman sat at the edge of the bench with her head leaned against the snack machine as if she was extremely tired. It was obvious that she had been there for a long time. There were two windows available for customer service and a door next to the soda machine, which only opened with the ringing of a buzzer, operated by the person behind the window. I walked up to that window which was in the path directly in front of me. There was a uniformed police officer sitting behind the window. May I help you, he suggested as I approached. Yes, I replied as I was digging into my purse to retrieve the paper holding the information that was given to me at the hospital, which included the name of the police officer that was handling my daughter's case. May I speak with Detective Armstrong, I replied. Do you have an appointment he asked? No, I replied. I would like information regarding a case that involved my daughter. Do you have written permission from your daughter to obtain information on this case he; asked. My daughter is deceased, I replied. She passed away a week ago. I would like information regarding the accident that caused the death of my daughter. You see that window over there he said pointing to the window on the left, go over there, fill out a request for a police report, pay ten dollars to the clerk and you can receive a copy of the police report which will give you the information regarding the accident. I walked over to the window and rang the buzzer on the wall. A clerk came to the window and asked me what I wanted. I would like a copy of a police report I replied. Fill out this form with as much information as you can and return it to me with ten dollars. I took the form and walked over to one of the benches and began to fill it out. When it was completed I retrieved ten dollars from my purse and handed it all back to the clerk. You can come back to this window in two to three working days to pick up your report she replied.

Back at work everyone watched me in curiosity, but no one dared to question me about the details of my daughter's death. I tried hard to drown myself in the daily processing of paperwork, the constant ringing of telephones and the heavy load of filing that was piling up in the file box while trying to ignore the whispers that were going on in the surrounding cubicles while everyone pretended to ignore my existence. I was new to the company no one really knew what type of person I was, where I come from or what my family life was about. That was the coldest Monday I've ever witnessed in my life, but in a strange kind of way I appreciated the fact that everyone left me alone. I appreciated the fact that no one questioned me regarding the details that lead to the death of my daughter. I realized that they either didn't know what to say or didn't want to say the wrong thing although they all were bursting with curiosity. Finally it was five o'clock. I had to pick up the baby from the learning center. I still had no idea what to tell him or how to comfort him. I knew that this would be another night that he goes to bed crying for his mother. The part that saddened me the most was the fact that I realized that he understood everything that happened. He knew that he would never see his mother's smiling face again, never feel the warmth of her body close to his, she would never get another chance to kiss him good night and that he would never get a chance to kiss the tears as they rolled down her cheek. He knew that his mother was never coming home again and there was nothing that I could tell him to ease the pain that he was feeling deep within. I knew that this would be just another quiet night for us. Another night the television played for hours, but was never really watched. Dinner that was prepared, but sat cold on the table because neither of us had an appetite. We spend hours just waiting for the sun to set so that we could go to bed and hope for a better day tomorrow.

As we lay in bed, I cradled him within my arms as I had done many times before, but this time was different. He held me just as tightly as I held him and he wept silently. Then I heard a small whisper from beneath the covers Mama, he called. Yes baby, I replied. Everyone has a mommy and a daddy right? Yes, I replied as I braced myself for the next question. I know my mommy is in the sky with Jesus, but where is my daddy? Why is it that I don't have a mommy or a daddy? I took a deep breath. I wasn't sure how to answer that question, but I knew that I had to answer it with much thought. Daddy will be back I replied he had to go away and get his thoughts together, but he will be back don't worry.

When I woke up that morning I knew that it would be just another day at work that I placed no effort and no interest in the job, another day that I would be just going along with routine. No one said anything to me except good morning until someone approached me from behind, put their arms around me and whispered, it's gonna be alright. The voice quickly registered in my memory, but I couldn't turn around just then because I was suddenly overwhelmed with reality. I fought hard to keep the tears from falling from my eyes, but it was of no use. Kimberly placed her cheek next to mine and repeated it's going to be all right. I sensed the gathering of bodies at the entrance of my cubicle, but I did not want to face anyone and witness the sympathetic look upon their faces. I couldn't speak. There was a lump in my throat about the size of a baseball. Kimberly tried to carry on with her normal cheery personality as she asked, girl what are you doing here? You should have taken some more time off. Don't worry about money; I'm going to pay you regardless. Girl, go home! Still unable to speak I just waved my hands, shook my head and began typing on the keyboard. Then I felt two warm hands on my shoulder blade. I saw the reflection in my computer and I knew that that was Tanya. She paused for a long while and then she spoke. I'm sorry she said. I wasn't trying to be cold, but I didn't want to make you cry again. If there is anything you need, just let me know. I shook my head and just sat there for a while. I tried to gather myself but suddenly found that I had lost the ability to function. I needed a moment alone so I reached into my purse and retrieved a pack of Salem Lights and a cigarette lighter then I headed for the outside. I walked a circle around the building and in my mind asking why, Lord, why. I returned to my desk hoping that no one else would come in to console me. All I wanted to do was get lost in the daily shuffle of paperwork.

As the days went on it became easier to cope with the situation, but I still didn't want anyone asking me questions about the details of my daughter's death because I had no answers. It was Friday already and I needed to occupy another lunch hour going to the precinct to retrieve the police report. Maybe once I read the police report I can answer some questions.

I walked into the precinct and rang the bell for the clerk. May I help you she replied as she approached the window? I requested a police report several days ago and I was wondering if it was ready I replied. The clerk took my driver's license for identification and walked away from the window. When she returned she handed me three pieces of paper. The first sheet entitled "incident/investigation internal copy" consisted of nothing more than my daughter's name, location of accident, detective name and description of vehicle involved. The second sheet consisted of nothing more than a three-lined typed statement that indicating that my daughter, after arguing with her husband, opened the vehicle door and jumped as the vehicle was traveling fifteen to twenty five miles per hour. The third sheet gave my son-in-law's name and the description of the car. I looked up at the clerk in confusion. This is it I asked. This is what they call a police report?

This is what I paid ten dollars for? This doesn't tell me anything. Can I speak to Detective Armstrong? She motioned me towards the other window and said you have to request to speak with him over there. I walked over to the other window and requested to speak with Detective Armstrong. Have a seat over there the police officer pointed towards the bench and walked away from the window. After a while a police officer appeared from behind a double door and called, Ms. Williams. I stood up and approached the officer. Follow me, he said and he turned and re-entered the double doors. There was another desk there where the officer requested to see my identification. The first officer turned towards me and said I am detective Armstrong, what can I do for you? I would like more information regarding the death of my daughter I requested. Your daughter committed suicide he replied. No she did not I argued my daughter had been threatened by her husband upon many occasions one of which is recorded by DePaul Medical Center I continued. My daughter did not commit suicide I argued. Detective Armstrong interrupted me and said, I am not concerned with what happened before the accident my only concern is what happened at the scene. Your son-in-law stated that your daughter opened the car door while he was driving and exited the vehicle while it was in motion. Your daughter did not live long enough to give her statement therefore; we can only go with what we have. He concluded the conversation by assuring me that the case has been placed in the "cold case" files and it will not be reopened unless you have any additional information or proof that would lead us to believe that this was foul play. Good day Ms. Williams, he said as he turned and walked away. The police officer at the desk handed me my driver's license and motioned me towards the door. I watched as Detective Armstrong disappeared down the hallway. I was angry and confused. Somehow the words "cold case file" sent a chill through my whole body. How could nothing else matter? How could they not consider all the calls to 911? How could they not consider the medical report? How could they not consider the fact that my daughter's body had no scratches, no scrapes, no cuts, no bruises and no broken bones? How could a person jump from a moving vehicle and come out clean?

It was obvious that the police was very unconcerned. I knew that I had a long journey ahead of me in proving my daughter's death. I had already made up my mind that this was not the last time that the police would hear from me.

I knew that Marcus was going to Florida for a while. What I didn't know was that he would return driving a Lexus. My mind began to wonder how could he not have money to bury his wife, yet have enough money to purchase a car? It was obvious that he was very confident in freedom as he expressed the same phrase that the police quoted to me, "the burden of proof is on you" he said as he turned and walked away.

It has been a month now that LaChelle has been buried and I needed to do some research of my own. I needed to know how a mentally healthy person could suddenly decide to commit suicide in the amount of time that it takes to prepare a grilled-cheese sandwich. Although people have gone back to their normal life-styles they were still having a hard time coping with the fact that LaChelle is no longer with us and we all wanted answers. What happened to the energetic, vibrant person that we were all familiar with. Her life had just reached the peak that every girl dreams of. Marriage to her high-school sweetheart, the uniting of her son and his father, a new home, a new environment, and to heighten her pleasures she had just learned that Philip was about to become a father. The idea of her first niece or nephew placed her in the position of planning the baby shower. It was just a few weeks ago that she stood in the mirror practicing what she'd like to be called; Auntie, Auntie Chelle, Auntie Ladybug or Aunt Chelle and just few weeks ago, to amuse herself, she was gathering materials and plan-ning a baby shower. It was just a few weeks ago that she received her income tax return just in time to put a down payment on her car. It was just a few weeks ago that she was beginning to feel that her troubles were coming to an end because Marcus has just two more weeks before he begins his out-processing with the mil-itary. Hopefully in about two weeks he'd be gone. It was just a few weeks ago that, even through her problems, LaChelle was beginning to spring back to life, planning the baby shower of her first niece of nephew, sitting in bed reading sto-ries to her son or singing and dancing to the tunes from the radio. All of that is gone now, never to return.

As I sat at my desk staring into the computer I realized that my mind was not at all on the assignment that I was supposed to be completing, I was anxious to get home because I needed to surf the internet; I needed to write some letters, but I had no idea where to begin. I started making phone calls. Who is Detective Armstrong's boss, and what is the ladder of command within that particular police precinct. I was guided to the chief of Police. I purposefully addressed a well-detailed letter specifically detailed every active moment since my arrival to the state of Virginia. I outlined every single previous incidents of domestic vio-lence, attempted murder and 911 calls making it very plain how this all played out to end up with a possible murder that was obviously being totally ignored and recorded as a suicide. I received a reply reminding me that I was not involved, that this is between husband and wife, that I do not have the rights to access the information in question, and because I don't have any new information regarding the "actual crime scene", that there's nothing they can do for me. Once again I was assured that this case was closed and would not be reopened.

My heart was bleeding and my soul was not at rest. There is no way I could let my daughter lie in her grave without answers. I needed to write more letters, so I continued with the City Mayor, District Attorney, Assistant District Attorney, Lawyers, Congressmen and Senators. Each reply was basically the same. Each reply led me back to the office of the Chief of Police.

Dear Ms. Williams: I sympathize with your concern; however, this is a matter that is decided at the city level. I have forwarded your correspondence to Norfolk's chief of police who has jurisdiction over this matter.

Dear Ms. Williams: The city Attorney's office defers to the professional judgment of the Police Department investigators because investigation is their area of expertise. Therefore, this office is not in a position to direct the Police Department to reinvestigate a closed matter, even though you may have reasons to believe that a criminal investigation is necessary. Please accept our condolences.

Dear Ms. Williams: Unless there is new information or evidence, the commanding officer of our detective division feels that re-opening our investigation would not be productive.

Dear Ms. Williams: State law, conflict of interest rules and other policy considerations prohibit this office from providing legal representation or advice to an individual citizen. The Commonwealth's Attorney's Office investigates and prosecute criminal offenses. Under Virginia Law, it is within the prosecutor's discretion whether or not to institute an investigation.

I couldn't control the rage that built up within me. Investigation? What investigation? No one did an investigation and how will they ever know if I have new information because no one will even speak with me. With the on-set of this aggravation, I decided to take my affair to the media only to find that the local news carriers does not have freedom of the press and can only report what is authorized by the office of the Chief of Police. With no place left to turn, I pursued to outside sources.

Dear Oprah, Montel Williams, Maury Povich, The Donahue Group; I have a show idea for you. It is called "Nobody's Job". Dear Al Sharpton, Jesse Jackson, NAACP. It was the infuriation of receiving the same response every time that caused me to retaliate even further. Dear President Bush, Vice President Dick Cheney, U.S. Department of criminal justice Services, Secretary of Defense, Secretary of State, Department of Defense, F.B.I., Bureau of Investigations.

Dear Sir: Thank you very much for your reply to my letter. I understand that you hold a very tedious position and you are very busy, therefore I promise not to take up any more of your time. However, I must tell you that I am disappointed, but not surprised that you did exactly what everyone else has done. I guess when you do the same thing you're expected to get the same results. For almost two years now I have been requesting for someone to go beyond the day of the accident in order to understand where I am coming from, but that has become the impossible task. I promise you, should we never speak again until we meet on the doorsteps of heaven, it will be then that I <u>will</u> prove you wrong. Thank you for your efforts.

And in the midst of it all, I stood in the courtroom after requesting custody of Marcus Junior and listened to the judge tell my son-in-law that in the state of Virginia "grandparents have no rights", therefore "It is up to you", he continued "whether or not you even want this woman involved in this child's life". Then he looked at my lawyer and said, "Counsel, could you please tell your client that in my courtroom she has no voice, therefore I don't want to hear anything that she has to say". I feel as if I'd just been bullied, raped and robbed by the legal system and there is nothing that I could do about it.

Moving from the North to the South was definitely a culture shock. It didn't take long to add this move to my worst mistakes of a lifetime list. I couldn't understand how a State so beautiful, so peaceful and so friendly could be so heartless, so cold, so unconcerned. The "commonwealth" was something I'd never even heard of until I moved here. I feel as if I'd left the real world and landed a major role in an exaggerated drama movie on the Lifetime channel. This is the only state I know of where you can get fired from your job by your co-worker simply because Virginia is a "right to work" state, your landlord can make you homeless simply because Virginia is an "at will" when everything is said and done you just must realize that "this is the commonwealth and that's just how it is in the commonwealth". Sometimes I wonder what progresses Martin Luther King really made. Money is the only object of success. Everything ranging from stealing a pack of gum to murder is legal depending upon whom you are or whom you are associated. The Chief of police has the authority to make the decision whether or not they will or will not investigate a crime, and obviously domestic violence is not a crime. Did you say "America, land of the free?" Not in the commonwealth!

I thought 2000 was a bad year, but here I stand five years later with both hands in the air saying "Lord, where do I go from here?" What now? How in the heck did I get into this situation? I don't think I'm familiar with this person that is occupying my body's capacities. I'm hoping for a miracle because I know that only a miracle could possible straighten out this mess. For some reason I was under the impression that "United States" meant that we were all somehow connected to one union. I was under the impression that, when the slaves were freed, that meant all people. I am well aware that state laws differ from state to state, but in an overall category I was under the assumption that freedom was freedom as long as you abide within the constitution of the United States. Boy was I wrong!

I WILL SEND A COMFORTER

I am leaning on God's promise that he would never leave us nor forsake us. Perhaps it was taking me too long to heal; therefore he had to send more than one comforter.

It was bedtime but it wasn't late. I wasn't quite sleeping and neither was I fully awake when I heard Chelle's voice as she called to the vehicle that stood in the distance, see you later, she waved excitedly. From the shape of the front end of the vehicle it seemed to be a limousine, white with a shiny grill and shiny rims. Perhaps I didn't notice the back portion of the car because my main focus was on the highly energetic young woman dress in white from head to toe who was extremely anxious to be home. I heard the key as it slid into the lock and then the closing of the door. While my inner sense alerted me that I'd buried my baby a month ago, my motherly sense was overcome by a strange calm that let me know that I could go to sleep now because my child is now safely in the house.

People keep telling me to let it go. You have to let it go they'd say it's the only way you're going to heal. You have to go on with your life; Chelle would want it that way. How do I tell this to the three-year-old who often asks if we could go back to the house with the steps that goes up and up and up. I knew what he was asking, but how could I explain that going back to new York was not going to bring our happiness back and neither is it going to bring his mother back. Although this child was young, he had a broad understanding of the entire situation. I know that his little heart is now broken in a million un-repairable pieces and there is nothing that I could do about it.

Today is Sunday and I was on my way to church but since I had to pass the graveyard I decided to stop by the gravesite first. The gravediggers were busy preparing a plot for another funeral. I watched as the backhoe digger scooped dirt from the large hole in the ground and placed it on top of a pile next to it. The weight of the truck caused the tires to sink into the ground as the claw lifted and dropped soil. I couldn't help but place my hand on my heart as a sharp pain paralyzed me for a moment. How on earth is my child supposed to breathe with that machine sitting on top of her chest, I thought? The workers must have noticed my facial expression because he came over to comfort me. Are you okay he asked?

I was too choked up to speak so I waved my hand, got back into my car and sped away. I tried to drown myself in the service, but all I could think about was that heavy machinery on top of my child.

After several month of exhaustion I realized that two to three hour of sleep was going to eventually wear me down quickly, but it didn't matter how much I tried to get my life back on track sleeping just seemed to be the impossible task. This particular evening the house was extremely quiet, probably because no one was there but me. I'd exhausted all forms of entertainment. There was nothing of interest on the television, I was tired of listening to the radio and I'd played every C.D I owned until I couldn't stand to listen to them one more time. So I lay across the bed. I wasn't at all tired, but I knew that I needed to try and get some sleep so I could go to work tomorrow. Suddenly the room became extremely cold. My past experiences alerted me that a certain spirit had entered into the atmosphere, but I didn't know whom it was or what to expect because I no longer had control of my body. I felt my spirit lift from my body and connect with the familiar spirits that surrounded me. I was led to a vehicle in which I also recognized. There were two people sitting in the front seat. I knew exactly who was in the front passenger seat as I reached forward to touch the blue-tinted hair of Sis Thorpe. Before her death I regarded her as my grandmother. She turned around enough for me to catch a glimpse of her beautiful smile as she looked over at the woman in the driver's seat. Mama, I exclaimed in amazement as Chelle lovingly placed her head on my shoulder for a quick hug and said, Mommy I'm going to show you where I am so you don't have to worry about me. As we began to disappear into the clouds I noticed that there was no back end to this vehicle. We stopped at a place that looked as if we were deep in the midst of the forest. The trees were a healthy green and it was extremely quiet. This is where I have to stay for a few weeks Chelle said, there's something that I have to learn before I can move to the next level. Suddenly I arose from the bed, wakened by the spirit that re-entered my body, I stood in amazement in the middle of the floor, raised my hands and raised my head towards heaven and cried out, Thank you Lord, Thank you. My soul was satisfied and my mind was at ease. I was thankful that the people I loved were caring for her.

Once again, it was just one of those days. Although I had no particular reason to be sad, unhappy or depressed, I was overcome by an overwhelming crying experience. Perhaps it was brought on by the vision that I carried the night before. Just as I was beginning to believe that I was headed towards an end to this madness I found myself standing in a beauty salon. This particular beauty salon I had never entered before, yet there's a sense of familiarity in the air. I wasn't there to get my hair done, neither was I there to get a manicure or a pedicure, in fact I wasn't there for service at all. As I was standing in the door-way viewing the world outside I realize that I'm in this salon simply because it is a safe-haven settled in the middle of a shopping center in the midst of a very rough neighborhood which is very unfamiliar to me. I know I need to leave this salon and I am trying to leave, but fear engulfed me to a point where I am literally paralyzed. This overwhelming feeling was telling me that there was something outside waiting to devour me and I knew that the only thing separating me from life and death was a glass door. Nobody seemed to mind my presence, in fact, they all seemed to be aware of my situation and they understood the position that I was in, yet no one was willing to extend a helping hand or even a suggestion. They just watched and waiting to see how I was going to resolve this. The bus stop wasn't far away and I could clearly see the bus coming. I was aware that the bus was my way out and I had fare in my hand but I was frozen to that position.

People were coming and going, passing me by, getting in their cars and driving away. Some even nodded or offered the gesture of a friendly smile. A certain car, black in color, encircled the monument in front of the salon; around and around it drove as the passengers inside kept their eyes on me awaiting my exit. Across the way I see a frail female, very sad and helpless sitting in a chair tilted on the hind legs leaning against a brick wall. Although I'd never spoken with her, somehow I knew her story. Her life carried the same scenario as mine. One day she'd found herself in the same situation, the same neighborhood, and the same beauty salon. Her life as it is today reflects her exit. The moment she stepped outside she was overpowered and devoured by the outside world that awaited her. She was physically hurt really bad, sexually abused and left to drown all alone in her own sorrow. Not crazy, but angry. Angry because people who knew her position and had the ability to reach out to her chose to watch her decay rather than offer a ride to safety. She prayed time and time again that her life would end so that the pain would stop, yet she sat alone, aimless with no place to go. The surrounding industry seemed to be carrying on business as usual. No one else seemed to be disturbed by the surrounding scene.

Business is coming to a close. The sky is darkening. The last customer was about to pay for her services. I'm doomed. I watched the owner of this salon as she prepared to close up the shop and depart. In my mind I knew that she too would pass me by, get in her car and drive away. Yet I'm still positioned in the doorway staring at the bus stop; so close but yet so far. The bus hasn't come all day and those thugs are still patiently pacing.

Just then the conviction of reality entered my spirit and I realized that I was the girl leaning against the wall. It's up to me to denounce the spirit of fear and the spirit of loneliness that has overcome me. The glass door was the protector that God has placed between me and all those demonic spirits that was threatening my exit. All I needed to do was trust past my own understanding and know that there is hope if I just take the chance. The thugs were my own insecurities and the reason why the bus has not arrived is because God is waiting for me to get over my fears and trust enough to come to his depot. I looked down in my hands as I held my fare and realized that I have all I need right here in the palm of my hand. My journey of salvation will begin the moment I take that first step of faith.

A GOOD SOLDIER

During the ten years that I was a military wife I never knew of a plan created or enforced by the military to help the spouses or the families of an enlisted experience comfort during their travel other than to serve the soldier at their level of self-satisfaction. During that time there was no such thing as the Automatic Spousal Life Insurance Policy, as a matter of fact, there was and still is a phrase within the military community, which quotes, "if the military had wanted their soldiers to have wives, they would have provided one in his duffle bag".

While everybody thinks being a military spouse is so grand, let me tell you that it all depending upon what type of mate you're were married to. The military offers many incentives to their soldiers to encourage marriage such as the family allotment, which raises and sometimes almost doubles their paycheck. Many soldiers, especially low ranking soldiers leap happily at this opportunity paying little or no attention to the love that is suppose to make a marriage special. The bible states that a wife should submit to her husband, but it doesn't state how far that submittal should go. I've seen so many wives beat, burned, physically and sexually abused in the name of submittal. I've come to realize that when you find yourself married to the wrong man, he spells submittal "S.T.U.P.I.D." This was usually the occasion with soldiers mainly because the military acknowledges their spouses to be "dependants" which mean, the soldier are totally and single-handedly responsible for their spouses and through human nature it seems that when a person finds themselves in "total control" of another person, the person in control automatically and unwillingly become overly possessive.

Within the military community it was natural for wives to fish through the lives of their neighbors and lay the dirt upon the table to the wives that just arrived in the community. This was the moment to sort out who's who and what's what. Gossip was the only skill many of these women possessed and they perfected the art of using it well. I had only been there a few days when, while standing at the bus stop with my children I was warned about the woman living directly across the hallway from me. "Don't become friends with her, she's very weird. No one is a friend with her and her badass children. Her husband beats her all the time, they steal, the kids curse uncontrollably, I think the whole damn family is crazy". Suddenly I found myself surrounded by several wives issuing warnings in one manner or another about this family. I had no idea who this family was that she was speaking of, I haven't yet seen this woman or her children, but I was sure that I was soon to find out exactly who it was that they were speaking of. It wasn't long before the whispering started and fingers were under-handedly pointing to the little Mexican woman walking towards us, "there she is, that's her". I peered over my shoulder at the small-framed woman standing about four feet tall as she looked towards me and smiled. She stood quietly with one child in her arms and two standing next to her as she waited for the school bus. Her eyes peered very uneasily at the other women. When the bus arrived she escorted one child up the steps and turned and walked back towards the two-story building in which we resided. I couldn't help but notice how harmless, hurt and lonely she seemed to be. I've been a military spouse now for six years, so I know how this game is played.

A few days later I was unpacking a box when I received a knock at the door. There stood the little Mexican woman with the baby in her arms and a frail child half-hiding behind her. Hello, she said in a very friendly, very soft voice. My name is Maria. I live across the hall there she said pointing to the door directly in front of me. I saw when you moved in a few days ago and I just wanted to intro-duce myself. This is Victor she said looking down upon the child who was now looking up at me with the prettiest smile I've ever seen, and this is Hector Junior she politely mentioned motioning to the baby in her arms. Hello I replied as I reached out to Victor for a handshake. My mind automatically reverted to the warning that I had received at the bus stop. I sensed that she wanted to come in and talk so I figured, what the heck, invite her in. Would you like to come in for a few minutes I suggested, I was just trying to unpack some things. There wasn't much hesitation as I widened the door and stepped aside allowing her access to the apartment. Of course nothing got unpacked instead we sat for hours getting acquainted with each other. I learned that her other son was the same age as Philip. Oh, perhaps they are in the same class she suggested. I'm waiting for the school bus to come pick up Victor; she continued, he's in special Ed and he only goes to school for four hours a day. I was curious as to why, but I thought the relationship was too young to ask. Somehow I knew eventually that question would be answered. How long have you been here I asked? I've only been here for three years. Do you like it? It's O.K. she replied. We hadn't been talking for more that a half hour when I noticed the fidgety child was becoming extremely hyper. It wasn't hard to notice that this woman had no control of her children. Sud-denly Victor arose quickly and began running around the room, jumping on furniture, touching the stereo, messing with the television, looking in boxes. Maria began to look very annoyed as her voice grew louder and louder. Victor come here she demanded. Victor began to laugh uncontrollably as he ran around the dining room table. Come here, come here she kept calling. Victor ran into my daughter's room. I followed in curiosity as he slid under the bed and exited the other side as she reached for him running then into Philip's room. He jumped across the bed and snatched a car from the nightstand as he passed. Maria finally caught him by the collar. With one uncontrolled child by the collar and the other screaming in her arms she dragged him back into the living room where she began to apologize for his behavior. Finally the school bus pulled up in front of the building. Maria's face relaxed with a sigh of relief. Victor swung the front door opened and darted outside. The lady that was standing at the bottom of the steps lifted her pointer finger into the air as she caught eye contact with the overly hyper five year old. Victor immediately stopped, tucked his hands tightly at his side and walked slowly towards her. He stood still for a moment until he was motioned to step up onto the bus. The natural sweet innocence of a child suddenly took control of his frail body as he was led into a seat. As the school bus pulled away, Maria exhaled with another sigh of relief. Victor is very hyper she began to explain with a timid voice of embarrassment, he takes medicine for that but I didn't get a chance to give him his medication this morning, but that's okay because they will give it to him at school. I became very curious about the woman that I am now facing and began to wonder if I should have taken the advice that I was given and push this woman out of my life. For understandable reasons, the conversation that took place at the bus stop kept taking control of my entire thought process. I've always been the type of person who took pride in discovering people and personalities for myself, but I don't think this was the type of person that I'd like to associate myself with, perhaps I'd be better off if I just stayed to myself.

That was just the beginning of a three-year relationship between Maria and myself. Maria's husband was extremely abusive and Maria was not permitted to discipline her children. Her husband had ordered the children not to obey their mother simply because she was a female and his reasoning was that a female did not have the authority to control a male. Hector Sr. was very aggressive, very rude and very bold. Maria had been married to him for ten years and within that time she had three children and several miscarriages. Miscarriages because her husband beat her so badly that she lost the babies over and over again. Hector was in control of the entire family's being. I realized that the children's uncontrollable behaviors were due to the anger they had to endure from day to day. He sometimes ordered the children to gang-fight Maria when he sought that extra ounce of entertainment. If he felt that they were not doing a good job, he would join in the charade. It was hard to conceive that a five-year old and a seven-year old was so extremely revolting, not only towards their mother, but also towards each other. I know that many people believe that boys are supposed to be rough, but this was over and beyond the limit. There were times when I feared for the life of one of those children as well as Maria. The baby was so frightenly adjusted to the entire situation that even from the high chair his personality was beginning to show signs of violence as well. It was normal for him to throw a temper tantrum so fiercely that the chair would shift from its original position. He had become so accustomed to having everything snatched from his little hands, that when food was placed before him, he would cram as much into his little mouth and hold tight to the rest in his little fist for later consumption. Even at this tender age, he realized that he could control his mother by throwing, screaming and kicking. I felt so bad for Maria that there were times that I would stand inside my apartment, hearing the thrashing from her apartment and just pray for her safety. I couldn't understand why no one seemed to be doing anything about it; it was as if nobody cared. Was everybody so accustomed to this behavior that it didn't really even matter or was it better that everyone ignore it all. Upon several occasions Maria would come to my house to call her husband's company commander, knowing that he was going to resolve the situation by telling her that Hector was a good soldier. It was of no advantage. Maria was a military wife and according to the military, she was Hector's dependant, therefore she was his personal property. During that three-year friendship I watched as Maria tried every thing she could think of to make the military deport her or send her back home, but nothing was good enough to bring on such a punishment. One day Maria went into the Post Exchange decisively to steal as much as she could carry in her pockets, tucked in her bra and up the sleeves of her jacket hoping that security would detain her. Since the security guard did not make motions, she approached him and opened her jacket to give him a clear view of all the items that she had collected as she brushed pass him and casually walked out the door. He then grabbed her forcefully and dragged her into the security room where he made note of everything as she unpacked herself onto the table in front of her. The store manager then alerted the Military Police who in turn summoned Hector and informed him to come retrieve his wife who had just performed another unsuccessful escape attempt. That evening was horrific. I feared for Maria not knowing what type of punishment her husband possessed in his insane mind. I took my children and positioned us at the far end of my apartment so that I would not have to listen to the brawls from across the hall. Although I turned up the volume on the television I could not prevent myself from imagining the actions of my neighbors. In my mind I could view the boys positioned on the sofa in the living room having to witness their dad's punishment towards their mother. The next day Maria came over to speak with me. She was walking very slowly and I knew that she was hurting. Victor was his usual out-of-control personality as he ran past her and down the steps to the outside. I followed him, realizing that Maria was not physically able to do so, but he instantly came to a halt when I called his name. I suppose from the sound of my voice he realized that I was not going to chase him. Maria began to tell me how Hector tortured her for the most part of the evening and how he ripped the clothes from her body and slammed her against the plate-glassed window in the dining area while telling her how ugly she was, how he wanted everyone else to know how ugly she was and that no man would ever want to subject themselves to have to look at that.

Diagonally across the street was a woman named Jackie who had a twelve-year-old daughter. Upon befriending with her, I learned that she had been in Germany for the entire life span of her only child. As her story began to unravel I realized that her parents had never met their only grandchild. I was totally amazed because I would have never thought an American could love another country so much that they would remain there for so long with no physical contact to their families back home. I became curious and wanted to know more about her situation, so I pursued with questions. So, your mother has never physically met your daughter, I asked. No, she replied, she's only seen her in pictures. So your daughter doesn't even know any of her cousins, aunts or uncles? Nope. When do you plan to take her to meet them; I asked. I can't she replied. What do you mean you can't? My husband won't let me. My eyes widened as confusion distorted my entire being, Excuse me, what do you mean won't let you; I replied as she quickly interrupted with the explanation. I am his dependant and according to the military I can't do anything without his permission. He takes away my I.D. card when I don't do as he says and without my I.D. card I can't even go to the corner store. I can't get grocery and I can't get money from the bank. I have no reason to leave the house. My head started spinning. Oh, my God! What in the heck have I gotten myself into? I'm relatively new to this life that seemed so beautiful but yet holds the tales of legal imprisonment. You mean your husband has held you prisoner here for twelve years? Yep! Did you talk with his commander? Yep! And what did he say? He tells me that my husband is a good soldier. I know that you are new to this and all, she continued, but you will soon realize, just like the rest of us what you can and cannot do. My mother is so unhappy; she continued. My daughter only imagines what her grandparents are like. They send her Christmas cards and birthday cards, but they've never met her. I saw the stress begin to build up on her face as tears slowly rolled down her cheeks. I've tried to file for a divorce, she said, but JAG told me that only my husband could file for a divorce. There is nothing I can do until he signs orders for my release. I've spoken to his commander so many times and the fact that he's a good soldier is all that matters to the military.

If I wasn't severely disheartened already, I was surely pessimistic now. The simple concept of what I now have to face was drastically overloading my thought process. What if this happens to me? What if my husband holds me here in Germany for the next twelve years? I swore to myself that I would kill him in his sleep not caring what a good soldier he was. Knowing I will spend the rest of my life in prison would be better than this anyway. What difference would it make anyway? In actuality, I am already in prison. My mind kept reverting to her words, "Trust me, I've thought about killing him or even committing suicide but the thought of what would happen to my daughter is the only reason I'm still here. Who will raise her? She doesn't know anyone else. She would be completely at his mercy and I couldn't leave her like that".

I wandered back across the street depressed. What did my future hold? I figured it like this, if I were the best wife I could be, maybe I wouldn't have to go through those types of things. I was never the type of person that easily attracted friends, neither was I the type of person that enjoyed gossip, so I conclude in my mind to assumed that these women must have done something pretty dreadful to make their husband treat them in such a manner. I made up my mind that I was not going to be such a wife. No way, no how!

Vicky portrayed herself as an independent type of wife. Her husband didn't have the authority to tell her where she can go, when she can go, whom she can talk to or what she can or cannot wear. I thought I had finally met someone who was as clear-headed as myself, someone that I could relate and befriend with on a daily basis, someone who understood what it was like to be a free American. It all came to a crashing halt the day I asked her to accompany me to the base club. This was the known party spot for miles around. Of Course, she replied what time are we leaving? Oh, about eleven o'clock I answered. I'll be ready she assured me; by that time the kids will be in bed and sleeping. That was the night that Isaac had duty. Her son was in his last year of high school and her daughter was about twelve or thirteen years old. When I came by to pick her up it didn't take a rocket science to analyze the fact that she was stalling for time. She was finding everything that needed to be done right now and before we leave. She made every excuse as to why she had to do what she was doing right now. My body swayed to the music that was anticipated in my mind from the club scene as I waited while she stalled long enough for me to lose the mood. I realized that there was nothing stopping her from going to the club but the orders of Isaac.

While in the Commissary on day I met a lady by the name of Leslie who was having problems coordinating her shopping items, shopping cart and purse. I stopped a minute to help when I noticing that Leslie had severe burn marks on her right hand. After several months of getting to know Leslie I found that her condition was caused when her husband forced her right hand into a pot of hot grease. Good Lord, what would cause him to want to do such a thing, I asked. Well, she began, I was fixing dinner and I had the oil heating to fry chicken when he began arguing with me about some bills. When the argument escalated, through his anger he grabbed my hand and slammed it into the oil. I've been through so many surgeries and am now having to learn to use my left hand as compensation.

During my learning experience I found that there are many different types of wives, yet they all were invisibly fighting the same war. The war of freedom, independence and individuality and they all fought in a different manner. Besides the wives that absolutely dedicate all of their free time to getting to know everybody's personal business were the wives who had to call their husbands fifty five times a minute to assure that they were doing the right thing and was in the right place. It wasn't often, but occasionally you would find a wife who was truly independent and free to be a human being.

As my marriage evolved I guess I should have been grateful to realize that the only problem my husband had was a bad case of street-feet. He found everything in the world to do so he didn't have to come home. This recalls my mind to the time when I first became a military wife. My first assignment was Baumholder, Germany. I was coming from New York with a three-month old baby and I was excited about finally bringing my family together and under one roof. When the plane landed it was mid afternoon, about 2:30 German time. I was lost amongst people who spoke no English wondering where I should go and what I would do if my husband didn't come to pick me up. I thought we had already had these plans arranged, but suddenly I felt like a little child lost in a supermarket. Suddenly everything seemed much bigger than I, everyone seemed extremely busy scurrying from one place to another. I couldn't even ask for directions because I had no idea where I was, where I was supposed to be or where I was going. Pushing a stroller and dragging a bag I tried to find the pick-up location for my suitcase. My eyes searched the crowd of people holding signs, which enclosed the names of the people that they were there to pick up. Husbands and wives locking lips and arms around each other while children laughing excitedly at the presence of their loved ones. I walked up to the big silver desk that stood in the middle of the floor and began requesting information. I was obviously an American and the attendants spoke very little English. I was tempted to approach the man in the green uniform when I heard someone call my name from across the corridor. My husband didn't seem to be apologetic about being late; as a matter of fact he didn't seem to care at all except to gather the bags and keep walking. He had a friend with him whom he forgot to introduce, but I didn't care because right now I didn't know if I was angry or relieved to be found. I was driven to a little apartment that sat in front of a farm. I'd come to realize that I was on the economy which is a way of saying that I was in German housing, not military housing. Once my husband opened the door and released me into the apartment, he disappeared out the door with his friend. I'll be back he called over his shoulder as he skipped down the steps and into the car. Hours passed as I sat in this strange house with no television, no radio and a newborn for entertainment. It had to be about four o'clock in the morning when I heard the key turn the lock at the front door. How little did I know that this was the first sign of the street-feet that I was about to spend the next century experiencing. It seemed that we were moving every two or three years from one country or state to another.

Ten years later here we are in Augsburg, Germany when my children asked that famous question, "Mom, does dad still lived with us"? If only I could tell them the truth I'd tell them that their dad lived with women in every neighborhood who was waiting for his charm and companionship that he so freely offered, therefore he did not have time for us. By this time I had convinced myself that I didn't even care anymore and it was very obvious that marriage vows were nothing more than a group of words formed by somebody nobody knows for the purpose of having a legal license to a God-accepted sex life.

WHO WILL TAKE CARE OF ME

After dedicating such a large portion of my life submitting as a wife, followed by years of service as a single parent, I now find that the plans that I had for my future were incomplete and I possessed skills that were behind the times of technology. Now I have to dedicate my life to playing catch-up. I had no idea what college was all about, but I knew that this was something I needed to do. Thank God I have a child that was ambitious and determined to go to college even though she knew that mommy did not have any money to send her there. She knew that she had to find a program that would support her dream and mine. She also was aware that she had a child that somehow had to be cared for during the process of all of this.

Several years ago I had invested in a computer even though I really had no need for it, but since everyone else was getting one, why not us? In the beginning, this big clumsy looking machine was nothing more than a fancy typewriter. The time has finally come to discover the world of "the internet". I had heard about people surfing the Internet, but now I have to discover this for myself. I had no idea where to begin. Isn't it funny how the things you thought could never have an influence upon your life, suddenly becomes extremely important. I had seen scenes on television, in movies and commercials about people having a late start in life, but never in my childhood dreams would I have found myself in this situation.

LaChelle was determined that we could overcome these obstacles. She sat down at the computer and began plugging in websites, researching colleges, applying for grants, applying for loans, filling out application after application and form after form. She found out about programs that we never knew existed. Somehow I didn't mind her having access to all my personal information. Social security numbers, salary, date of birth, etc…

It wasn't long before I found myself working full-time days and in a classroom in the evenings. When I got out of class I would drive to LaChelle's school, which was about a mile down the street and pick her up. Together we would go pick up the baby from whom ever was caring for him that evening; hungry and tired we headed for home so we could prepare ourselves to do it again tomorrow. LaChelle spent the majority of her time during the day seeking a babysitter for the evening while we attended school. When I needed to do research, but found that I had no time she would sit at the computer and do that part for me. She was determined to help me get through this. She was determined that I was going to catch up with the times and she was also determined that her future dreams would not end up like mine. I know that it wasn't easy for her because she was in the same situation that I was in, trying to be a single mother while having to work and handle the pressures of finding a trust-worthy babysitter in a city where no one could be trusted. One thing you did not have to explain to me was the mental stress and the physical stress that came with the situation. Although she knew that I would always be there for her, she was still dealing with the realization that she was the main attraction in the life of her child. At 19 years old she found that did not have a life of her own. She wanted her independence as an adult, but she knew that it was going to take some time to get to that point. She was holding on to the dreams when she could bring her husband and child together and under one roof to make it holy in the eyesight of God. She was holding onto the hope that one day she could rekindle the relationship with the father of her child and perhaps they would get married and connect their family as one. She often spoke of a home involving two working parents and perhaps a brother or sister for her already existing son. All she wanted was the average American dream, nothing fancy, and nothing extreme, just the average American dream.

LaChelle was always there for me. She took care of me. When I was sick, depressed or lonely I could always count on her to pick me up. Sometimes even without words, she sensed that I was down and knew just what to do to revert my mood. One day she came home from work holding a bag that labeled the name of the local ninety-nine cents store. Inside the bag was a small statue. Nothing much, just something to say, I thought about you today. There were times when I felt guilty when I fussed at her about things that I thought she wasn't doing right. I often warned her about the type of friends she associated herself with. She had a habit of denying herself for other people if she thought she could be supportive in some way. I often warned her that people would take advantage of her kindness if she weren't careful. My previous relationship had made me confident in knowing that when I become an old lady, she would be there to take care of me. Often I would think of our relationship and how close we had become. The memory passed through my head the evening that I was lying in bed, the clock read 10:35 PM. The noise from the outside vibrated the walls in my bedroom.

Someone was blasting the song "Cupid" from their car radio. Knowing that this was LaChelle's favorite music artist and her favorite song, I envisioned her in her bedroom rocking to the beat. I waited until her favorite part began then I called out to her. Chelle, come here a minute. I giggled to myself because I knew that I had interrupted her moment of pleasure to ask her to do something dumb. You called me all the way in here just to ask me to turn off your light she replied as she sucked her teeth, rolled her eyes, flipped the switch and turned to go back into her room. As the song continued to play and I heard Chelle becoming deeply mesmerized by the lyrics, I called again. Chelle! What, she replied. With a snicker I called, could you bring me a glass of water? I heard her huff as she headed towards the kitchen. She knew that I was discovering ways to enjoy aggravating her simply because her favorite song was blaring outside. Somehow I felt that she was finding enjoyment in my antagonizement. With one hand on her hip and the other wrapped around a glass of water she stood in the doorway with and annoyed half-smile upon her face. I knew that she was waiting for me to start laughing because the song had finished and the radio rang out with commercials. Living in New York you learn to live with many loud noises. She handed me the water, rolled he eyes and walked back towards her room. My mind searched for a reason to call upon her again, but I knew that she wouldn't come this time, so I decided to simply go to sleep. I thought I was dreaming when I heard her voice beckoning me to come. Hurry Mom she squealed. The sound of her voice let me know that something was seriously wrong. My mind began to race. What was happening? Was there something going on outside? Was it something on the news? Was it something she found? I quickly leaped from my bed and raced down the hallway. My curiosity was racing faster than my feet. What happened I asked as I approached the doorway? She looked up at me from her bed and replied could you turn my light off please.

How could God have taken away such a beautiful relationship and left me sitting here empty-handed, alone and angry. A huge portion of my soul was missing and I knew that it was gone forever. I was angry with myself for even asking God to end the madness. Had I known that he was going to act this manner, I would never have prayed that prayer. Should I now be grateful that he sent an immediate response?

Another Sunday that Satan has stolen from me. For the past few Sundays, I would rise, find a church, plant myself there for the morning service, evaluate the congregation, the choir, the ushers and the Pastor, then decide if I even wanted to connect myself permanently to the environment. Not today and not this Sunday, instead I woke up with a pen and paper in my hand preparing to write an obituary. In between thoughts and memories, I was sweeping, mopping, dusting and gathering laundry because I knew that within the few days my home would be crawling with family. I need to use this Sunday to search the yellow pages to find an undertaker, a burial ground, and a preacher, pick out a coffin, chose a burial outfit and locate a church. And the reality of it all is that I know that I will be doing this all by myself. Philip and his fiancé had already arrived. They met me at the hospital the day before as we stood together by the bedside of his sister and watched as life slowly drained from her body. My heart was enlightened when I saw a small tear roll down Chell's left cheek because I knew that somehow she had gotten a prayer through. I knew at that moment that she had prayed her last prayer. My heart sunk, but I wasn't going to give up hope until I heard the words "she's gone" come from the mouth of the medical staff. My entire world had suddenly become unusually quiet, a sort of quiet that I had come much too familiar with, the sort of quiet that let me know that this was the calm after the storm. I was consumed with feelings that I had never experienced before and I really didn't know how to handle them. I didn't know if I wanted to be proud of my daughter for defending herself the way she did against the man that she vowed to love forever or if I should have told her to give in for the sake of saving her own life. I knew that had she submitted to her husband as the bible instructs her to do, she would have been subjected to this abuse for the rest of her life, besides, what would it matter if I had told her that or not if the life insurance policy was what he was seeking anyway?

I remember when I was a little child growing up in New York, my parents had taken me to Coney Island, an amusement park which was introducing a new ride. This attraction was called "The Hell Hole" and was featured as the thrill of a lifetime. This was a big cylinder where you walk inside and place yourself, standing up against a wall. There were no belts or buckles to hold you there during the motion of this course, just your own body weight and the force of the world around you. The ride would begin to spin. It started out slow then got faster and faster. Suddenly, the floor would drop and you'd find yourself stuck to the wall from the pressures of mere air. The only thing you were fighting against to release yourself was gravity. But gravity had such a stronghold on you that you couldn't as much as pull your head from the wall. The object of the ride was to try and free yourself, however this never happened until the floor returned and the spinning slowed. Wow, what a rush! This is how life had become for me. As if I was permanently on the Hellhole. All forces were against me and I had no chance of freeing myself. But just like my daughter, I knew that if I wanted to survive I had to fight. I too, am in a fight for my life. Satan is now the gravity that's holding me up against a wall. My floor has fallen out and the spinning in not ceasing. Lord, for how long will I be on this ride? Is it that no one seems to care or is it that they are all fighting their own hellhole? Am I going to fall before the floor returns? Is this my revelation? I wish that there were a way that God could give me another life, another chance, another opportunity because I've messed up so badly with this life that my whole existence seems to be totally pointless. Sometimes I ask myself, am I going through one of life's seasons or am I just hollow? Does anybody see me out there? I realize that more things are accomplished through prayer than the world gives prayer credit for and it seems that God had been leading me all along. Has he been speaking to me at times when I haven't heard? It took me all these years to realize that God was in my life long before I opened my heart to him. My hellhole was now spinning out of control. The bottom had fallen out a long time ago. Can someone please help me get off this thing? I know that I complained about the roller coaster of life, but I'll take the roller coaster now, thank you!

I turned on my computer in an effort to get started. I pulled up an outline of a church program that I had typed about a year ago for my sister's fiancé. I had typed programs so many times for the church, but never did I think I would be using this same outline to complete a program for one of my own. I had the basic information, name, and date of birth, educational level, name of parents, brother, cousins, aunts and uncles on my side of the family. I then hung the obituary on the refrigerator to be completed by for her father's side of the family. When the obituary was completed I stood back and counted. A quarter of the page listed family members and I couldn't help but think, where were they all when she was screaming for help? Where were they when she was begging for a hiding place? I couldn't help but to think how this all could have been avoided if one person had shown a little concern a few days ago, a week ago or even a month ago. I guess I really don't have a right to be angry. It's not like I know how it feels to belong to a family anyway. Being raised in the foster care system, all my life I've been a member of a group of people who calls themselves "family" but never failed to let me know that I was not a "family member". Then I married into a group of people who calls themselves "family", but sought ways to let me know that marriage did not provide me with rights to enter into their little circle. Non-acceptance was surely something that I could relate to and I realized that my struggle had carried on to my daughter when she researched the background of her dad's family while trying to understand their customs, she called her aunt over to our house for a cooking lesson in their native tradition. All she wanted was to be connected to someone or something.

Today I called to speak with little Marcus. It was Thanksgiving and I just wanted to tell him Happy Thanksgiving. He was at the restaurant that his grandfather owns. There was so much noise in the background that I could hardly hear him. It was obvious that the restaurant was very busy. I couldn't help but think how this restaurant wouldn't even exist had my daughter not died. I guess you could say I was a little upset although I didn't know whom I was upset with. I don't know if I was upset with God for allowing this business to be successful or if I was upset with that family who seems to be so proud of themselves for what they are accomplishing, upset with the law for placing my grandson in that situation as if they were snickering at the death of his mother by smashing pie right across his nose or am I just upset because I feel so helpless.

It's been three and a half years now since I've buried my daughter and the pain still strikes me as if it just happened yesterday. It seems so unfair. They get a thriving business and I get to clean my baby's grave. Whenever I need to remind myself that this is not just a nightmare I go out to the cemetery. I make it a point to stand directly on top of the spot where my daughter's body lay. The hard cold ground beneath my feet is a constant remainder that this is the reality of domestic abuse. I read the headstone over and over again, LaChelle Williams-Harris, Mother, Daughter, Wife, July 30, 1980-June 22, 2002. I had many dreams for her, but never did I think these dreams would end with her name carved in stone. I often think of how charming the sound rang in my ears during my pregnancy while trying to choose a name for the beautiful little creature growing inside of me. Rubbing my stomach and connecting by heart strings to this little bundle of joy that I couldn't wait to hold in my arms and love forever, LaChelle Tonea, what a beautiful name. I often think about the day I brought her home from the hospital and how I'd lay her upon the bed, undressed her to count all the rib bones, toes and fingers. Amazed that she was so absolutely breath taking, the little miracle that God had presented to me as a gift and the best gift I could have ever received. There is nothing that any of us could do for her now and as far as I am concerned, it is finished!

DEAR DAUGHTER:

I'm glad I didn't get a chance to say goodbye.
Often I sit and think of the times when you were a little girl
playful, elegant and full of joy.
You knew that you had life in the palms of your hand
And you lived it to the full extent.
When you became a teenager
No one but no one could take the place of your mother
and you made it a point to let me know this
I watched the twinkle in your eye grow brighter each time we shared
those precious moments together, Just you and I
I watched you grow, love, live, learn and cry
but never did I think I would have to watch you die
No more trips to the mall
No more wrestling across the living room floor

Daughter, I want you to know that
I felt you when you came back to say "I Love You Mom"
I smelled you when you came for a hug
I heard you trigger the alarm on my car
I'm happy to know that
although we are not together physically,
spiritually we are still connected

Kiss Mama for me, Kiss Sis. Thorpe for me,
Hug Snowman and tell Uncle William that
I said "Thank You"
One day God will bring us all together again

That's why I'm glad that I didn't get a chance to say
Goodbye.

Love, Mom

THAT'S ME

Just because you can't see me doesn't mean that I'm not there
I, too, must find ways to let you know that I care

Each time you see the lights flicker, that's me
Each time a paper falls to the floor for no apparent reason, that's me
Each time you hear a faint noise that only you could hear, that's me
Each time the wind catches you within the hug of it's whirl, that's me

Just know that I am now your guardian angel
I've seen every tear that you've shed
Heard every prayer that you've said
I know the loneliness unheard

But Mom, remember that I am not dead
God has borrowed me to do a mission on the other side
I have to prepare a place for angels to abide
but in between my time of toil, I am with you

You might not see me, you might not feel me
but I have you cradled within my arms
I watch you as you sleep
I comfort you when you weep

And when that honored day arrives,
The day when God calls you home to rest
I will be here, waiting

Hand in hand
Heart to Heart

Arm in Arm
We will be together again

Until then, Mom
Please don't cry
Maybe you can't see me,
But I definitely have my eyes on you

Love,
LaChelle

ABOUT THE AUTHOR

Jessie Thompson is the youngest of nine children born to the single parent household of Fannie Mae Thompson in Greenville, South Carolina. She was four years old when her mother was murdered and was then transferred from home to home through the foster care system until she settled in Bronx, New York where she grew up.

She began her writing career at about ten years old. After supper, while the rest of the family sat before the television, she was often found at the kitchen table with the radio low, equipped with a pen and paper where she taught herself to write short stories and poems.

Two years after High School graduation she married and traveled in and out of the United States with her soldier husband for ten years. In 1990 she separated from her husband and returned to New York as a single parent.

After the nine eleven terrorist-attack on New York in 2001, she lost her job and decided to relocate to Norfolk, Virginia for a new beginning. Three months later, after burying her only daughter, she found herself all alone in a state that was very unfamiliar to her. Because her fight for justice led her through many avenues of failure, she decided to use her talent to put her testimony in book form. She knows that she can no longer do anything for her own child, but prays that through her testimony, the life of someone else's child might be saved.

978-0-595-39236-0
0-595-39236-9

www.ingramcontent.com/pod-product-compliance
Lightning Source LLC
Chambersburg PA
CBHW030354290526
45785CB00004B/1749